ARMORED STRIKE FORCE

THE PHOTO HISTORY OF THE AMERICAN 70TH TANK BATTALION IN WORLD WAR II

Charles C. Roberts Jr.

STACKPOLE
BOOKS

Lanham Boulder New York London

Published by Stackpole Books
An imprint of Globe Pequot
Trade Division of The Rowman & Littlefield Publishing Group, Inc.
4501 Forbes Boulevard, Suite 200, Lanham, Maryland 20706
www.rowman.com

Distributed by National Book Network

Printed in the United States of America

Library of Congress Cataloging-in-Publication Data

Names: Roberts, Charles C. (Charles Chester), Jr., 1944–
Title: Armored strike force : the photo history of the American 70th Tank Battalion in World War II / Charles C. Roberts Jr.
Other titles: Photo history of the American 70th Tank Battalion in World War II
Description: Mechanicsburg, PA : Stackpole Books, [2016] | Includes bibliographical references.
Identifiers: LCCN 2015039359 | ISBN 9780811717656
Subjects: LCSH: United States. Army. Tank Battalion, 70th—History. | United States. Army. Tank Battalion, 70th—Pictorial works. | World War, 1939–1945—Tank warfare. | World War, 1939–1945—Regimental histories—United States.
Classification: LCC D769.306 70th .R62 2016 | DDC 940.54/1273—dc23 LC record available at http://lccn.loc.gov/2015039359

Contents

Introduction

THE 70TH TANK BATTALION served in North Africa, Sicily, France, Belgium, and Germany from November 1942 to May 1946. It was organized as a medium tank battalion on 5 June 1940, redesignated as a light tank battalion on 7 October 1941, and after 1 December 1943 ended the war as a standard tank battalion with medium tanks. In the beginning at Fort Meade, the 70th was instrumental in developing armored tactics, testing new equipment, and writing the book on armored warfare. In North Africa, the 70th fought against the French, with the French, with the English, and against the Germans and the Italians. During the entire North African campaign, the 70th developed the fighting skills that served it well until the end of the war, including its first amphibious combat landing in Operation Torch.

The 70th then invaded Sicily, performing its second amphibious landing during Operation Husky near Gela. It fought from Gela to Palermo, encountering the more formidable Panzer III tanks and defeating them with innovative top attacks from nearby hills. After Sicily it was off to England, where the battalion arrived at Liverpool to prepare for the cross-channel invasion. In England, the 70th trained with other units and participated in practice landings during Exercise Tiger. The unit was instrumental in developing new devices for the invasion at Utah Beach, including amphibious tanks. On D-Day, 6 June 1944, the 70th was the first armored unit to land and move inland to relieve airborne troops and consolidate positions. After the capture of Cherbourg, the 70th moved on to the pivotal battle at St. Lô, opening the way for General Patton's Third Army's dash across France. During the summer of 1944, the 70th rolled across France, through Paris, and into Belgium and Luxembourg in pursuit of retreating German forces. After surviving the Hürtgen Forest campaign, the 70th was instrumental in the counterattack against German forces during the Ardennes offensive (Battle of the Bulge). Crossing into Germany, the 70th headed southwest, battling rapidly retreating German forces and ending the war in the vicinity of Munich.

This book functions as a pictorial history of the World War II years in the eastern United States, Morocco, Algeria, Tunisia, Sicily, England, Normandy, Northern France, Belgium, Luxembourg, and southwestern Germany, from the perspective of the 70th Tank Battalion. Rarely is such a wealth of photographs available of as small a unit as the 70th. Almost 600 photographs appear here, a number more typical of the histories of divisions or armies. Most of the photos provided did not have captions, explanations, or dates. Consequently, various clues in the photographs, such as vehicle type, weapons, uniforms, and terrain, as well as information from documented photos from other works of the same subject, were used to generate captions for these photographs. In some instances, other historians familiar with the particular theater of battle provided captions. Finally, while not all photos are accompanied by detailed captions, they are presented here for the benefit of other historians and readers of World War II history because of their high quality or the unusual material pictured.

CHAPTER 1

The Beginning: Stateside

FORT MEADE

Beginning in the 1930s, U.S. military doctrine held that independent tank battalions were to be attached to infantry divisions to support troops by bringing mobile machine guns and light cannons to bear on enemy infantry targets. In June 1940 the 70th Independent Tank Battalion was formed at Fort George G. Meade, Maryland, under the command of Lt. Col Stephen G. Henry. Shortly after, Henry was transferred to the Armored Force Headquarters at Fort Knox, Kentucky, to fulfill the need for officers familiar with armored unit operations; he was replaced by Maj. Thomas N. Stark, a former infantry officer. Because of materiel shortages plaguing the U.S. Army at the time, the unit was equipped with obsolete M2A2 light tanks when it began training in the summer of 1940. Later that summer, regular army officers were transferred to the 70th from other units, forming the core of the initial command structure. President Roosevelt reviewed the officers of the 70th at Fort Meade in September 1940.

The first draftees arrived in November 1940 and started basic training. In January 1941 Company A traveled to the Fort Indiantown Gap Military Reservation in Pennsylvania for qualification in various aspects of tank warfare. The company used up their annual ammunition allowance during this training, to the displeasure of the War Department, which was sensitive to the ammunition shortage. In early 1941, officers and enlisted men of the 70th attended the armored school at Fort Knox, where they trained in rapidly changing tank warfare strategies influenced by the exploits of the German forces in Europe. Since the 70th was one of the few qualified armored units, the battalion was constantly giving demonstrations on armored tactics. Among the observers was Gen. George C. Marshall, chief of staff of the U.S. Army and close confidant of President Roosevelt. It was not unusual for personnel of the 70th to transfer and form the core of other new units, including the 1st Tank Group at Fort Knox. The 70th was often involved in testing new military equipment being developed by the armor board.

70th headquarters (the "L" stands for "light tank battalion") at Fort Meade. TAYNTON

Pvt. Joseph McAtee at Fort Meade circa 1940, with obsolete Renault-designed FT-17 light tanks made under license in the United States. MCATEE

Pvt. Joseph McAtee at Fort Meade inspecting an obsolete Mark VIII Tank, circa 1940. MCATEE

Harley Davidson WLA motorcycle. TAYNTON

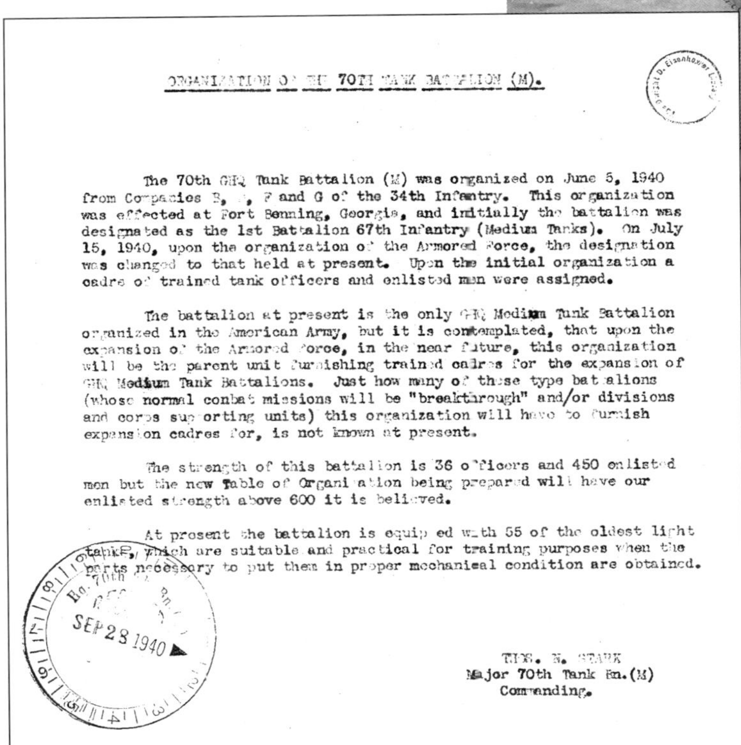

ORGANIZATION OF THE 70TH TANK BATTALION (M).

The 70th GHQ Tank Battalion (M) was organized on June 5, 1940 from Companies B, [illegible], F and G of the 34th Infantry. This organization was effected at Fort Benning, Georgia, and initially the battalion was designated as the 1st Battalion 67th Infantry (Medium Tanks). On July 15, 1940, upon the organization of the Armored Force, the designation was changed to that held at present. Upon the initial organization a cadre of trained tank officers and enlisted men were assigned.

The battalion at present is the only GHQ Medium Tank Battalion organized in the American Army, but it is contemplated, that upon the expansion of the Armored Force, in the near future, this organization will be the parent unit furnishing trained cadres for the expansion of GHQ Medium Tank Battalions. Just how many of these type battalions (whose normal combat missions will be "breakthrough" and/or divisions and corps supporting units) this organization will have to furnish expansion cadres for, is not known at present.

The strength of this battalion is 36 officers and 450 enlisted men but the new Table of Organization being prepared will have our enlisted strength above 600 it is believed.

At present the battalion is equipped with 55 of the oldest light tanks, which are suitable and practical for training purposes when the parts necessary to put them in proper mechanical condition are obtained.

SEP 28 1940

THOS. N. STARK
Major 70th Tank Bn.(M)
Commanding.

Memorandum documenting the organization of the 70th Tank Battalion in September 1940. The 70th was originally designated a medium tank battalion, but since it was equipped with light tanks it was redesignated a light tank battalion on 7 October 1941 and had this designation until 1 December 1943 in England. EISENHOWER PRESIDENTIAL LIBRARY

It was customary to adopt distinctive insignia for new units in the U.S. Army. Various proposed insignia were developed and submitted to the U.S. Army for approval.

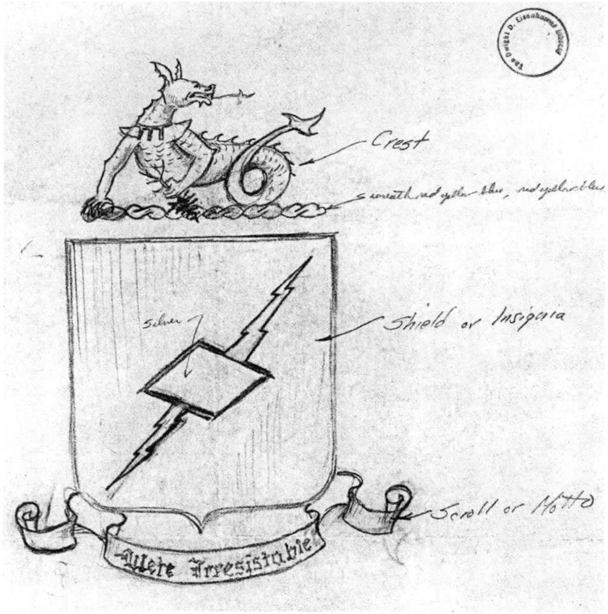

Proposed distinctive insignia from Koppers Co., Baltimore. EISENHOWER PRESIDENTIAL LIBRARY

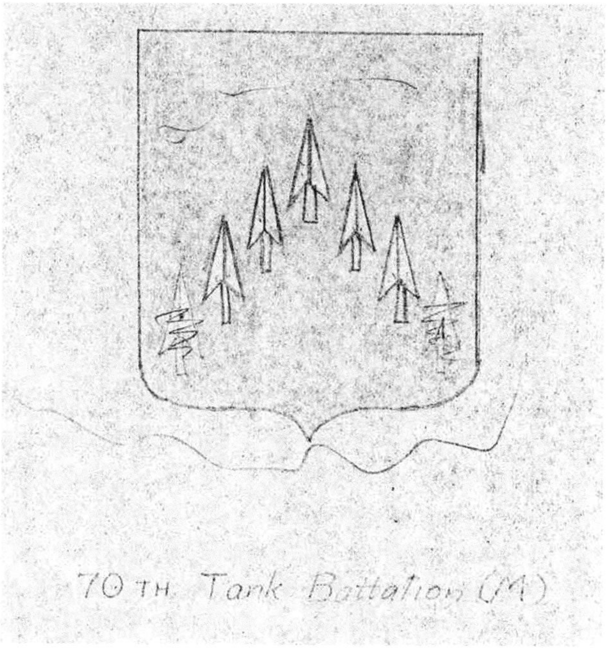

Proposed distinctive insignia from N. S. Meyers Inc., New York. EISENHOWER PRESIDENTIAL LIBRARY

The Tank Corps armored branch insignia adopted early in the war. ROBERTS

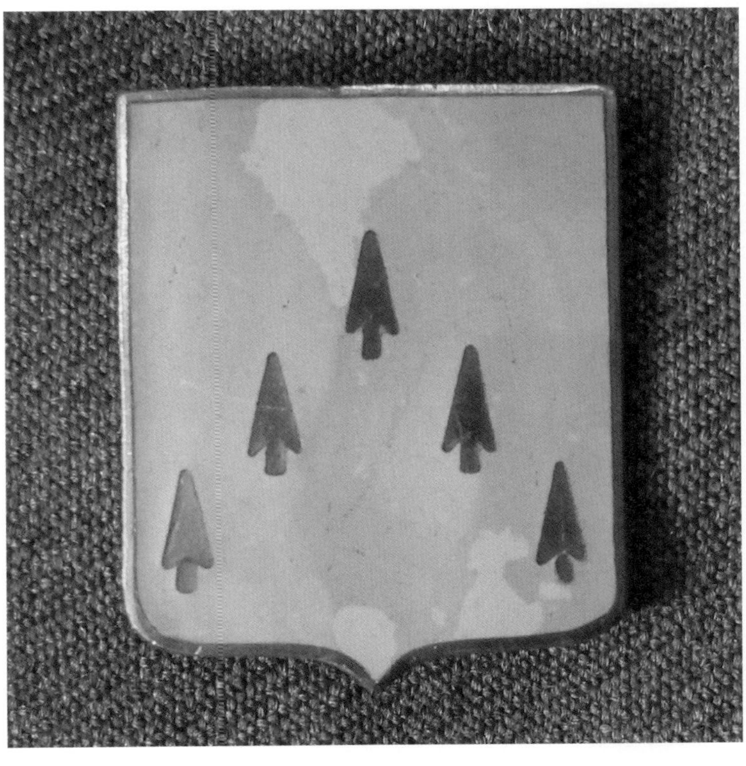

This distinctive insignia was eventually adopted. ROBERTS

Merry Christmas

December 25, 1940

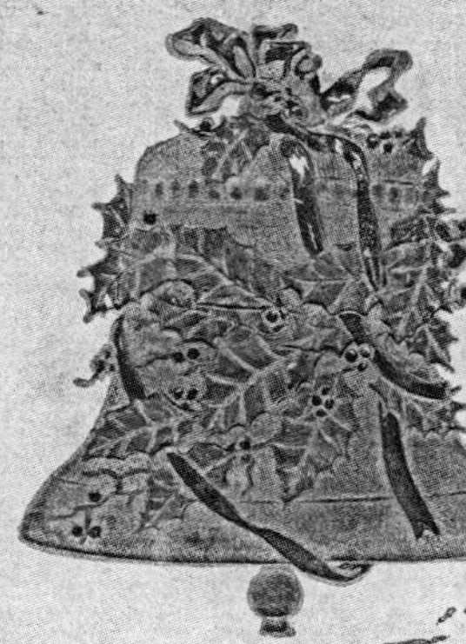

Headquarters and Headquarters Company
70th Tank Battalion (M)
Fort George G. Meade, Maryland

BATTALION HEADQUARTERS

BATTALION COMMANDER
MAJOR THOS. N. STARK

BATTALION EXECUTIVE
MAJ. THOMAS E. WINSTEAD

BATTALION ADJUTANT
MAJ. JOHN J. DUBBELDE, Jr.

PLANS AND TRAINING
CAPTAIN ROTHWELL H. BROWN

SUPPLY OFFICERS
CAPT. ARTHUR S. PETERSON
1st Lieut. ROBT. A. McKIRICHER

ASSISTANT ADJUTANT
CAPT. EDWARD E. CRUISE

PERSONNEL ADJUTANT
2nd LIEUTENANT MICHAEL C. VARHOL

HEADQUARTERS COMPANY

COMPANY COMMANDER
CAPTAIN JOHN C. WELBORN

RECONNAISSANCE
Captain Joseph M. Pittman
1st Lieutenant William E. Edwards
2nd Lieutenant Joseph H. Morgan

COMMUNICATIONS
Captain Thomas B. Evans

TRANSPORTATION
Captain Howard McC. Snyder
2nd Lieut. Olaf W. Christopherson

MAINTENANCE
Captain James E. Landrum
2nd Lieut. Edward M. Williston

COMPANY OFFICER
1st LIEUTENANT PAUL H. DAVISON

*

CHRISTMAS DINNER

Wednesday, December 25, 1940

Menu

*

Oyster Soup — Oysterettes
Celery — Lettuce
Roast Young Turkey
Cranberry Sauce — Sage Dressing — Giblet Gravy
Sliced Ham
Candied Sweet Potatoes — Snowflake Potatoes
Buttered Peas — Creamed Corn
Parkerhouse Rolls — Butter — Bread
Mince Pie — Pumpkin Pie
Chocolate Layer Cake — Fruit Cake
Apples — Oranges — Grapes — Bananas
Mixed Nuts — Assorted Candies
Coffee
Cigars — Cigarettes

*

ROSTER OF COMPANY

MASTER SERGEANTS
JOSEPH EICHNER
RAYMOND RILEY

FIRST SERGEANT
JOSEPH E. CURTIS

TECHNICAL SERGEANTS
JOSEPH F. ANDROS
ROBERT M. FOSTER
RALPH O. HARVEY
GEORGE L. MATEREWICZ

STAFF SERGEANTS
ROBERT F. FRIESE
POSEY B. HILL

SERGEANTS
George Barale
Joseph H. Bednarski
Karl J. Brown
Charles K. Carman
John J. Dukett
Adolph F. Grunsby
Bernard F. Henry
Fred J. Mandeville
Gordon W. Nelms
Bryan Popp
Russell B. Rhoades
Marshall J. Robertson
Anthony E. Schwoyer
Robert A. Williamson

CORPORALS
Russell C. Kautter
Hendrick A. Wansink
Frank Prepelka

PRIVATE FIRST CLASS
Stanley J. Angel
Ralph M. Arehart
James C. Benner
Carl L. Burney
George Cook
Elmer L. Corbett
Robert J. Crews
Ralph A. Dolfi
Alexander Eadie
George Furdella
Luther Gillis
Frank Grisafo
Aster Halcomb
Perry Hankins
Edgar P. Hendrick, Jr.
Luther Horning
Victor J. Hubany
Michael Hurchick, Jr.
Edward H. Kosmalski
Walter M. Lawhorne
Joseph V. Lescault
Alfred R. Lewandowski
William B. Lloyd
Edward L. Lynch
Richard F. McCoy
Leroy E. McDaniel Jr.

ROSTER OF COMPANY Continued
PRIVATES FIRST CLASS Continued
Thurman W. McDaniel
Harold H. Mengel
Roy E. Miller
Joseph Murray
Martin F. Polk
Thomas C. Pritz
Andrew B. Sulek
Robert E. Reams
Melvin T. Saffield
James R. Shelton
Andrew Sivak
Edward Stasiuk
Theodore P. Stempkowski
Henry J. Walsh
Belva F. Warf

PRIVATES
Allison A. Arrowood
William H. Ayers
Charles M. Barry
Julius A. Bartusick
Eugene Batdorf, Jr.
John W. Beckner
Daniel J. Bateman
Robert H. Bell
William H. Brothers
Henry W. Carroll
John A. Capobianco
Robert J. Connors
Earnie L. Daff
Lewis W. Donat
Foy D. Douthit
Hugh T. Drum
Louis Firlie
Frank R. Geist
Vincent Geonnotti
Frederick V. Gettz
David Hightower
Harold B. Hockman
Joseph L. Kanavey
Cecil W. Winburne
Benjamin F. Kincannon, Jr.
George A. Kint
Edward R. Long
Clarence E. Lucas
Joseph E. McAtee
John D. McDonald
Casimir S. Merchel
Arthur Micahel
Edward J. Nelson
Raymond H. Nunnemacher
Raymond J. O'Connell
Joseph Pimes
Burton C. Potter
George R. Reid
Harold M. Robinson
Roy D. Sheets
Edmund Thomas
Roscoe Thomas
Arrington B. Turner
John A. Ungerean
Samuel G. Van Horn
Benedict A. Vanyush
Earl R. Wells
Leonard Wolpe

Christmas dinner menu and a listing of members of the 70th Tank Battalion from 1940. EISENHOWER PRESIDENTIAL LIBRARY

A photo of a rare T2 37mm gun motor carriages (jeeps mounted with 37mm antitank guns) at Fort Meade. These vehicles did not become standard issue for the U.S. Army. TAYNTON

Early model T2E1 37mm gun motor carriage (Bantam BRC 40 jeep). Bantam Motor Car Company could not meet the U.S. Army demand for jeeps, so contracts were given to Willys and Ford to manufacture them. TAYNTON

View of early radio gear in a jeep. TAYNTON

Kelly Pool at Fort Meade, 1942. ERICKSON

Company A proceeded to Fort Devens, Massachusetts, where it was attached to the 1st U.S. Infantry Division. It took part in extensive training exercises in the Carolina Maneuver Area (Fort A. P. Hill in Carolina County, Virginia) until 2 December 1941, when the company returned to Fort Devens. In October 1941 the 70th was redesignated a light tank battalion. On 8 December 1941, just after the Japanese attacked Pearl Harbor, the newly promoted Colonel Stark, in a speech to the 70th, stated that the United States was at war. (It should be noted that the ranks of personnel in the 70th were elevated frequently due to wartime promotions.) The 70th was one of the few trained armored units and, upon the orders of the deputy chief of staff, Gen. Mark W. Clark, was given priority to receive ammunition, 37mm guns, and machine guns. At this time the 192nd and 194th Independent Tank Battalions were sent to defend the Philippines. If the 70th had been one of the battalions sent, its history would have stopped shortly afterward, since the 192nd and 194th were captured by the Japanese.

Once the armored vehicle was loaded on the end flatcar, it had to be driven to the front flatcar to make room for the next vehicle. TAYNTON

With all armored vehicles loaded, the 70th traveled to the particular maneuver area to which it was assigned. TAYNTON

Early war Dodge T202 VC5 $^{1}/_{2}$-ton truck at the 70th tank shop at Fort Meade. TAYNTON

A 1930s-vintage M2A2 light tank being loaded onto a flatcar for maneuvers. Flatcar transport was the primary means of armor movement since truck-drawn transporter trailers were in short supply. TAYNTON

Private McAtee next to a Dodge T202 VC5 $^{1}/_{2}$-ton truck in the motor pool at Fort Meade. MCATEE

Obsolete Mark VIII tanks in a storage yard at Fort Meade. These tanks were produced between World War I and World War II and were used to train armored units. Tank development in the United States between wars lagged behind that of many other countries. MCATEE

Obsolete World War I M1917 light tanks of French design (Renault) in a boneyard at Fort Meade. MCATEE

Doc Shechner. TAYNTON

Tank training at Fort Meade with the obsolete M2A2 light tanks, whose main armament was machine guns. TAYNTON

Training in the field continued with the 70th incorporating new vehicles and new doctrines in tank warfare. During 1940, truck and motorcycle transport were incorporated into operations performed by the 70th.

Motorcycle detachment training. TAYNTON

Beryman (the cook in white) eating a sandwich. This is a typical view of a field kitchen during training at Fort Meade. TAYNTON

Sergeant Wilt and Private Ainy. TAYNTON

World War I French 75mm model 1897 artillery piece plus caisson. The United States manufactured these cannons under license from France. They were mounted on half-tracks for tank-destroyer battalions and on M4 Sherman medium tanks. TAYNTON

A 1940 Dodge T202 VC5 $^{1}/_{2}$-ton truck. TAYNTON

A different angle of the 75mm M1897 gun. TAYNTON

Early model M2 half-track set up as a communications vehicle. TAYNTON

Early vintage 2.5-ton truck. This appears to be a GMC ACKWX-353. TAYNTON

Firing range with 1903 Springfield rifles, later replaced with the M1 Garand rifles. TAYNTON

A 1940 Dodge 1.5-ton cargo truck specially designed for the military with sturdy bumper and radiator guard. TAYNTON

Jeep being hoisted across a ravine during training, using a steel cable and pulleys. TAYNTON

The French 75mm gun had its undercarriage removed and was placed in the back of a half-track as a quick way to make a World War II tank destroyer. The pedestal in the center of the photograph held a .50-caliber machine gun. This vehicle was marginally successful and was later relegated to mobile artillery units. TAYNTON

Maintenance personnel installing track on an M2 light tank. The track came in eight-pad sections that were connected to links and installed on the tank. The track pads were rubber, which was very quiet while driving but somewhat hazardous on slippery terrain. TAYNTON

Early vintage M3 75mm gun motor carriages on flatcars on their way to a training area. These vehicles were half-tracks with a World War I–era French 75mm gun mounted in the back. This was the primary armored vehicle used by early tank destroyer battalions. TAYNTON

M2A2 light tank in operation as part of the maneuvers at Fort Meade. TAYNTON

Officer Candidate School (OCS) students inspecting an M2A2 light tank at Fort Meade. TAYNTON

Calibration of the machine-gun sights on an M2A2 light tank at a gun range. TAYNTON

M2A2 light tank loaded and on the way to a maneuver area. TAYNTON

Mule-drawn artillery (M1916 37mm gun) at Fort Meade in 1940. The M1916 37mm gun was used for training purposes but considered obsolete for combat. TAYNTON

Company C tanks training at Fort Meade. TAYNTON

Light tank M3 in operation as part of the maneuvers at Fort Meade. TAYNTON

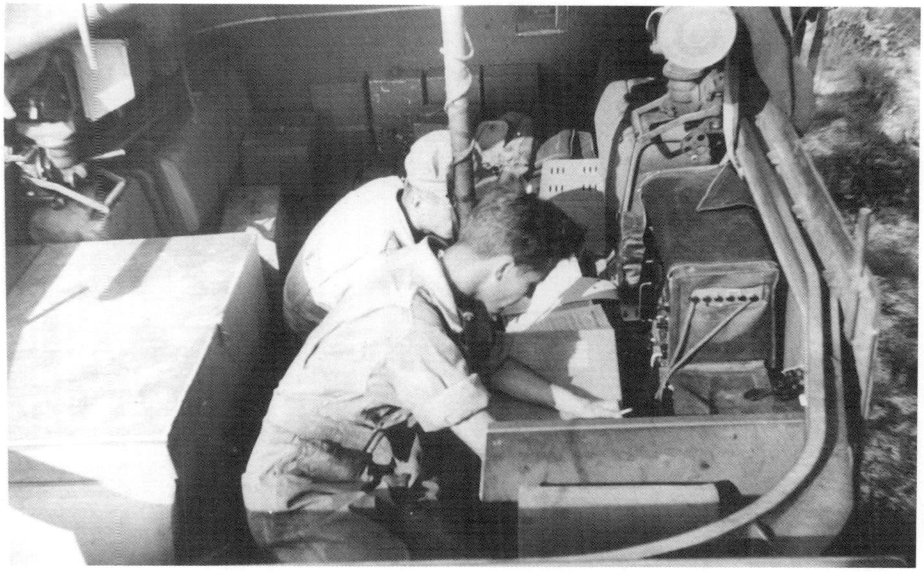

Communication equipment and operators recording messages. ERICKSON

View inside early half-track and radio gear. ERICKSON

The 70th tank platoon in training with M2A2 light tanks. DIXON

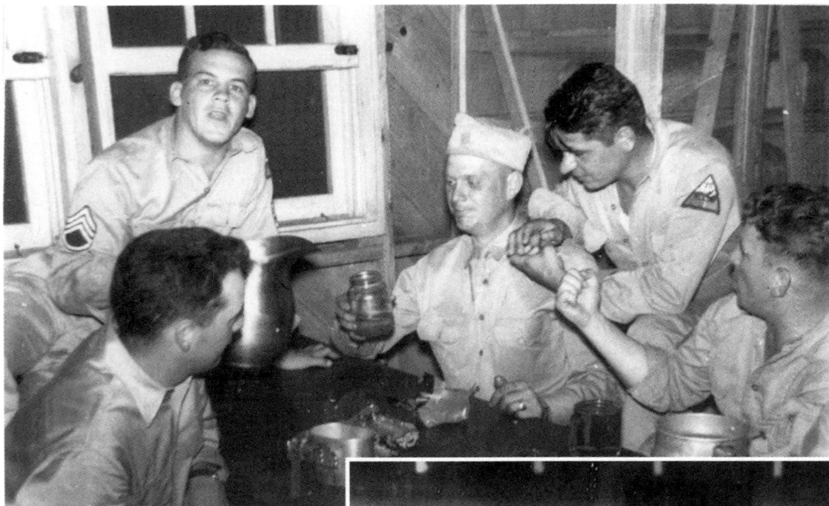

Typical barracks party with S/Sgt. L. C. Sproles at the upper left. Note the 70th Tank Battalion armor patch.
ERICKSON

The 70th Tank Battalion draftee football team, 1940–41, Fort Meade. Robert Connors is fourth from the left in the first row.
CONNORS

Robert Connors at Fort Knox, 1942, with photos of his sisters in the background.
CONNORS

Civilian Harley Davidson WL-series motorcycle at Fort Meade, 1942, owned by a T/5 of the 70th. ERICKSON

Front row (left to right): Windship, Robert H. Knoebel, and Riffle. Back row (left to right): DeLaney, Keating, Brighten, and Raburn. Basic training at Fort Knox, 1941. KNOEBEL

M2 half-tracks on flatcars proceeding toward maneuvers. TAYNTON

Dodge T202 VC1 command reconnaissance car. TAYNTON

Harley Davidson motorcycle with sidecar. ERICKSON

Early jeep and soldier with World War I helmet. TAYNTON

Photos of typical tank crew with new M3 light tanks. The new Herringbone Twill (HBT) coveralls are shown. Khaki uniforms had been used previously. TAYNTON

Training on new M3 A1 light tanks at Fort Meade. TAYNTON

FORT HOWARD

Main gate at Fort Howard, 1941. TAYNTON

While on temporary duty in 1941, Lt. Lewis C. Taynton visited Fort Howard, the headquarters for the harbor defense of Baltimore, Maryland. During his tenure in the 70th, he used his photography skills to take many of the pictures used throughout this book.

Fort Howard was constructed in 1896 and at the time of Taynton's visit was the home of Battery E, 4th U.S. Artillery. The fort was named after Revolutionary War colonel John Howard of the Maryland Continental Army. Douglas MacArthur commanded the fort from 1925 to 1928. During 1941, training of new conscripts was underway at the fort in preparation for possible involvement in World War II.

Fort Howard, Maryland. TAYNTON

Headquarters, 12th Infantry Regiment, at Fort Howard, a unit that would rejoin the 70th at Utah Beach as part of the 4th Infantry Division. TAYNTON

Fredericksburg Avenue (Fort Howard) looking at the post flagpole, 1941. TAYNTON

Typical gas station outside Fort Howard. Gas rationing was initiated during the war, with only a few gallons allotted to civilians per week. TAYNTON)

Officer Candidate School (OCS) formation. TAYNTON

A machine-gun crew firing .50-caliber weapons on a range at Fort Howard. They were still using the old M1917 World War I helmets, which were replaced by the M1 helmet later in 1942. TAYNTON

The 37mm antitank gun M3, a close copy of the German 37, was issued to the army in 1940. Many draftees were trained on these guns early in the war. TAYNTON

T28 half-tracks being transported to training maneuvers on flatcars. The T28 was the antiaircraft version of the M2 half-track, and was equipped with a 37mm gun and two coaxial .50-caliber machine guns. DIXON

Mortar, crewman, and ammunition. TAYNTON

M1917 Browning machine gun and crew during training. This weapon has a water-cooled jacket over the barrel that is connected to a reservoir. Notice the wooden .30-caliber Browning ammunition boxes. TAYNTON

Lew Taynton (kneeling) and fellow OCS students in summer khaki uniform with Stetson hats, some wearing Sam Browne belts. The Sam Browne belt was part of the uniform in the 1930s but became optional during World War II. TAYNTON

World War I–vintage small-caliber cannon (M1916 37mm gun) used in training at Fort Howard. Gunners are dressed in World War I–vintage helmets. This live-fire exercise was a rare opportunity to train with actual ammunition, which was in short supply. The observation tower is shown in the background. TAYNTON

M1916 37mm gun during summer training at Fort Howard. TAYNTON

SHERMAN FIELD

In 1941 Lieutenant Taynton went on temporary duty (TDY) to Sherman Field, Fort Leavenworth, Kansas. There he underwent orientation on the role of bomber aircraft in the combat tactics that the United States was developing in anticipation of upcoming hostilities. Taynton was given detailed training on the B-18 (Bolo), which the military was using at the time. The Douglas Aircraft Company developed the B-18 to replace the Martin B-10 as the Army Air Corps' standard bomber. The B-18 design was taken from the early DC-2 commercial transport. A total of 133 B-18s were contracted to be delivered to the U.S. Army Air Corps in January 1936. Several were destroyed during the Pearl Harbor raid. Because of inadequate engine power and defensive armament, the aircraft was relegated to training, transport, and shore-patrol duties.

Sherman Field, altitude 770 feet above sea level, formerly part of Fort Leavenworth. A twin-engine B-18 is parked on the tarmac next to the main hangar. TAYNTON

Multifunction control panel. TAYNTON

Lieutenant Taynton (right) and an instructor pilot (left). They are likely reviewing the aircraft controls and gauges. Notice the throttle handles between the two, which were used to adjust engine speed. TAYNTON

Lieutenant Taynton stands in front of Engine #1. Engines are numbered in ascending order from left to right, which is still done today. TAYNTON

Frontal view of a B-18, showing the bubble canopy. TAYNTON

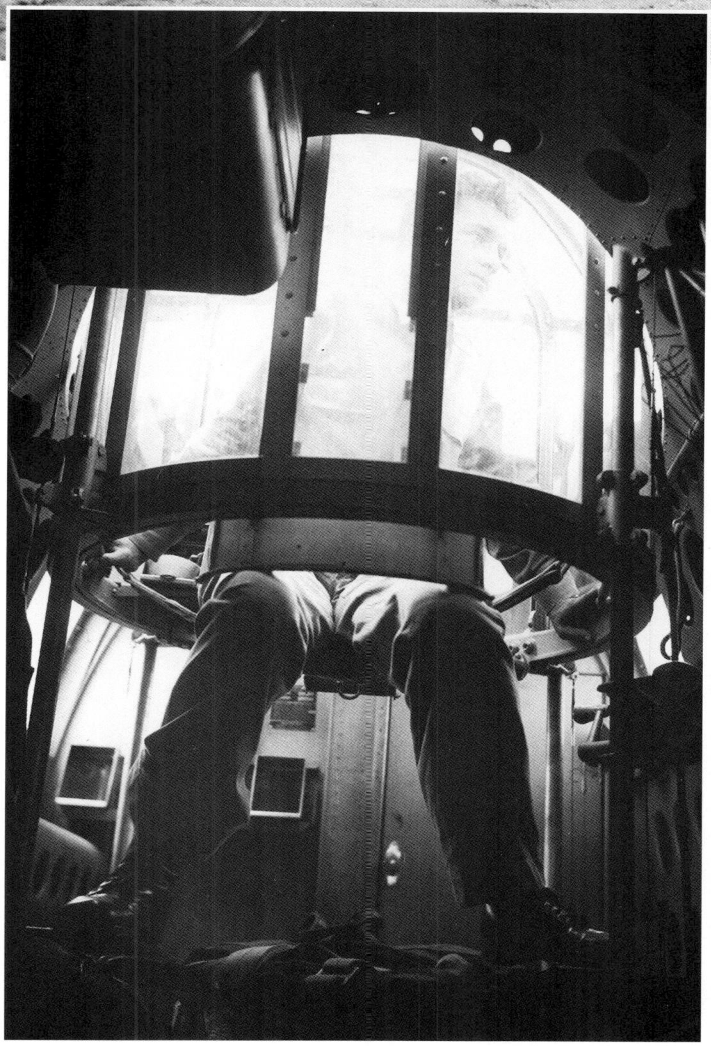

View of early turret in a B-18. TAYNTON

FORT A. P. HILL

In 1941 elements of the 70th traveled to Fort A. P. Hill (named after Confederate general Ambrose Powell Hill), at that time a newly developed military installation in Carolina County, Virginia. The 70th participated in practice maneuvers with II Corps and General Patton's Task Force A in anticipation of the landings in North Africa. This was often referred to as the Carolina Maneuvers.

Early Bantam Model BRC 40 jeep with an officer in the front-passenger seat and Sgt. John Dixon, the driver, Fort A. P. Hill, 1941. TAYNTON

Sergeant Newman having lunch in the field, Fort A. P. Hill. TAYNTON

Resting after all-day maneuvers, Fort A. P. Hill. TAYNTON

Sgt. John Dixon, Carolina Maneuvers, 1941. TAYNTON

A 1935 M2A2 light tank used in training by the 70th before and after the start of World War II. The M2A2 had two turrets, one for a .30-caliber machine gun and one for a .50-caliber machine gun. The M2A2 evolved into the M3 light tank and eventually the M5 light tank, which the 70th used throughout World War II. DIXON

With the fall of France and the installation of the French Vichy government, which collaborated with Germany, there was concern as to whether or not the French fighter aircraft squadrons stationed on Martinique in the West Indies were friendly. The United States had sold P40 fighter aircraft to the French prior to the war, and some of these aircraft were stationed on Martinique. The 70th was alerted to prepare for an amphibious landing on the island and to neutralize the threat, if necessary. On 9 January 1942 the 70th, accompanied by the 1st Infantry Division and 1st Marine Raider Battalion, sailed out of New York Harbor, through U-boat infested waters off the coast, toward Martinique. The threat of an invasion, accompanied by saber rattling from politicians, convinced the French to capitulate, rendering the invasion unnecessary. (Vichy France, formed as a result of the Franco-German Armistice of 1940 and partially under German control, became totally under German control in 1943. After the U.S. landings in North Africa, French units there changed sides and joined the Allies.) The convoy turned around and made a practice landing off the Virginia Capes. At this time the 70th was using the M3 light tank, an upgrade from the M2A2 light tank. The vehicle was slightly larger and equipped with a 37mm cannon.

M3 light tanks of the 70th in maneuvers practicing tactics. TAYNTON

Radial engine for the M3 light tank. This was a gasoline-powered aircraft engine, a Continental W-670, modified for tank usage. TAYNTON

Alex Sabo (left), a 70th Tank Battalion Company B crewmember, on an M3 light tank. MCATEE

M2A2 light tank mired in a ditch. Part of driver training was learning how not to get stuck. TAYNTON

Sgt. Anthony Tomasheski (left) and Sergeant Ferris (right) at the Carolina Maneuvers in front of their M2A4 light tank, November 1941. TOMASHESKI

Armored column including jeeps, half-tracks, and an early-vintage light tank. DIXON

FORT BRAGG

Arriving at Fort Bragg. TAYNTON

On 11 March 1942 elements of the 70th were transferred to Fort Bragg, North Carolina, for additional training with the 9th Infantry Division. Company C was transferred to Iceland to guard against a possible attack from the Germans. Colonel Stark was transferred to the Armored Force headquarters and was replaced by Maj. John C. Welborn. The obsolete M2A2 light tanks were exchanged for M3 light tanks.

Maj. Gen. Jacob Devers, chief of the Armored Force, visited the 70th Tank Battalion in early May 1942. General Devers later commanded the Allied force that landed in southern France in 1944 (Operation Dragoon). Company C, now stationed in Iceland, was redesignated the 10th Light Tank Company. (Part of the 10th Light Tank Company rejoined the 70th in England prior to the invasion of Normandy.)

In the summer of 1942, the 70th made several practice landings in Chesapeake Bay. Maj. Gen. George S. Patton visited the 70th in September 1942, giving one of his famous "tear the heart out of the enemy" speeches. New M5 light tanks arrived and were quite a change from the previous M3s. They had automatic transmissions that were easy to shift, two Cadillac V8 engines that ran well, and a newly introduced gun stabilizer that allowed the gunner to fire while in motion. Company A was attached to the 39th Infantry Regiment of the 9th Infantry Division. A reconstituted Company C was attached to the 60th Infantry Regiment, and Company B (less one platoon) was attached to the 47th Infantry Regiment. These elements were moved under strict surveillance and secrecy to separate bivouac areas on the Fort Bragg reservation. Pope Field was nearby and home to the newly formed elite airborne units. Despite the restrictions, many 70th tankers went into Fayetteville or Raleigh for R&R.

Company C, Iceland, 1942. U.S. ARMY

Lieutenant Taynton standing in front of an M3 light tank of Company A at Fort Bragg. TAYNTON

Lt. Gordon Brodie joined the 70th at Fort Bragg, North Carolina, in April 1942. He went on to command Company D in Normandy and Company A in France and Germany. He was one of the most highly decorated members of the 70th, awarded four Silver Stars, two Bronze stars, and the *Croix de Guerre*. BRODIE

Captains Michael C. Varhol, Edward L. Jones, and John M. Bushey. FRITZ

Lt. John P. O'Leary at Fort Bragg. TAYNTON

Early photo of Maj. John C. Welborn. FRITZ

Lieutenant Taynton, the soldier on the right, in front of an M5 light tank at Fort Bragg, North Carolina. TAYNTON

Lieutenant Taynton in an amphibious jeep (GPA). TAYNTON

A wrecker loads a fording kit onto an M5 light tank. This shroud allowed air to be drawn into the vehicle to run the engine and exhaust to be expelled. The 70th was assigned to work out the bugs in this new hardware. The fording kit was designed so that the tank could launch from a landing craft into water that would cover the hull but not the shroud openings. DIXON

Early M2 half-track set up as a mobile crane to lift the fording equipment onto an M5 tank. DIXON

New M5 light tank at Fort Bragg. TAYNTON

M5 light tank at Fort Bragg, 1942. This tank became stuck on a sand berm, providing the driver with a good training lesson on learning the intricacies of driving the M5. TAYNTON

M5 light tank and equipment laid out for inspection. ROSS

OFF TO NORTH AFRICA

Carrier *Yorktown* CV-5 departed Norfolk, Virginia, on 16 December 1941. The 70th was training in this area and Private McAtee probably snapped this photo before its departure. The blimps are antisubmarine patrols to protect convoys leaving eastern ports. It was common for German submarines to position themselves off shore rather than out in the Atlantic in order to torpedo departing ships. MCATEE

From September through November 1942, elements of the 70th loaded flatcars and moved from Fort Bragg to Fort Dix, New Jersey, in preparation for the invasion of North Africa. From Fort Dix they were transported to Staten Island and loaded onto transport ships, which sailed into the Atlantic. Among the ships transporting the 70th were the *Thomas Stone* and the *Susan B. Anthony*.

Attack transport USS *Thomas Stone* (AP-59). U.S. ARMY

Attack transport USS *Susan B. Anthony* (AP-72). U.S. ARMY

Officers of the 70th, Fort Bragg, North Carolina, 13 June 1942. TAYNTON

The following individual photos (shown in alphabetical order) of the original officers of the 70th show the date the photo was taken and the highest rank the men attained while in the military. The rank indicated on the photo is not the rank at the time the photo was taken. TAYNTON

Capt. William B. Bartholomew
6/13/42

Col. James A. Bender
6/13/42

Maj. John M. Bushey
6/13/42

Capt. Olaf W. Christopherson
6/13/42

Lt. Nicholas R. Corrado
6/13/42
KIA

Lt. Col. Henry E. Davidson, Jr.
6/13/42

Maj. William H. Dodge
6/13/42

Lt.Col. William A. Edwards
6/13/42

Lt. Gilbert G. Gault
6/13/42

Maj. Ira A. Hawk
6/13/42
KIA

Capt. Shull L Irwin
6/13/42

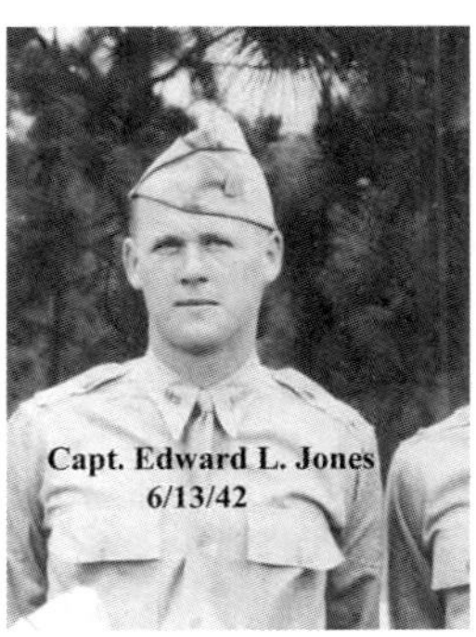

Capt. Edward L. Jones
6/13/42

Maj. Ralph V Lennen
6/13/42

Lt. Col. Robert A McKericher
6/13/42

Capt. James D. McLanachan
6/13/42

Capt. Joseph H. Morgan
6/13/42

Capt. John E. Mullen
6/13/42

Capt. Paul P. O'Leary
6/13/42

Lt. Col Jack J. Richardson
6/13/42
KIA

Maj. Charles D. Sammons
6/13/42

Lt. George H. Shaffer, Jr.
6/13/42

Maj. Charles R. Sharp
6/13/42

Maj. Lewis C. Taynton
6/13/42

Major Michael C. Varhol
6/13/42

Major Altee W. Wampler
6/13/42

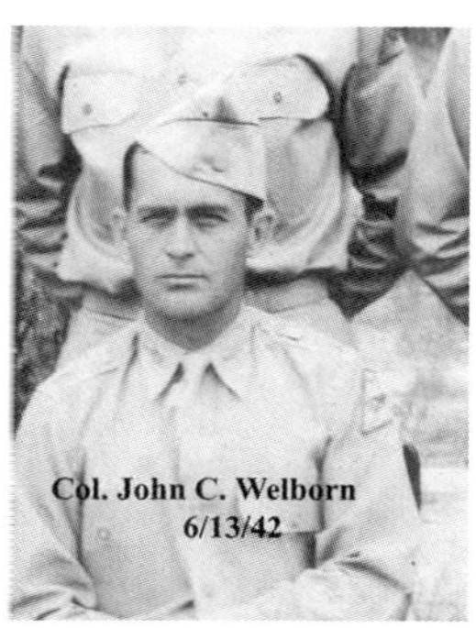
Col. John C. Welborn
6/13/42

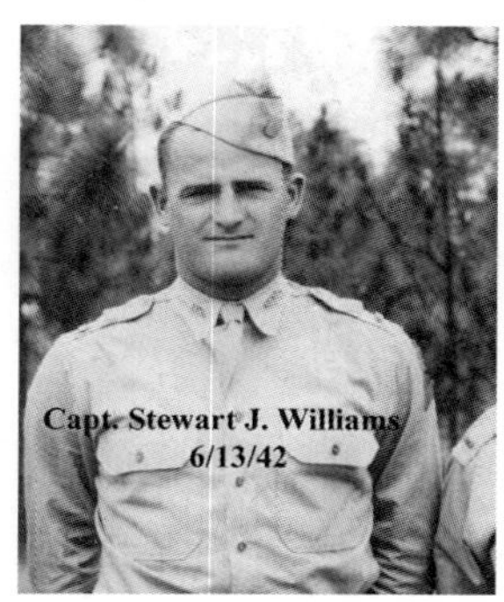
Capt. Stewart J. Williams
6/13/42

CHAPTER 2

Operation Torch: The Invasion of North Africa

THE INVASION FLEET, with advance elements of the 70th, arrived off the coast of North Africa on 7 November 1942 at Algiers, Safi, and Port Lyautey. A Company had sailed from England and arrived off of Algiers, having survived several aerial attacks upon entering the Mediterranean. B Company and C Company sailed from Norfolk and landed at Safi and Port Lyautey, respectively. At the time, North Africa was governed by the Vichy government of southern France, which collaborated with the Germans. Northern France was controlled by the Germans. U.S. officials thought that the French soldiers under the command of the Vichy government were not completely loyal to the Germans and could be persuaded to join the Allied cause, which eventually happened. The 70th, being an independent tank battalion, was split up and assigned to various units, including British and French.

USS *New York* (BB-34), commissioned in 1914, was Admiral Kelly's flagship during Operation Torch. TAYNTON

COMPANY A

Company A, commanded by Capt. Ralph V. Lennen, spread out on four transports carrying the 9th Infantry Division (USS *Chase*, USS *Stone*, USS *Leedstown*, and USS *Exceller*), landed at Algiers, Algeria, on 8 November 1942 during an enemy aerial attack. The *Stone* had sustained torpedo damage to its propeller and was later towed into Algiers. Soldier Francis F. Ross said that everyone on board the *Stone* realized they were a sitting duck for U-boats, but the tugboat arrived in time, saving the day.

Company A was attached to Combat Team 39. Company HQ vehicles included T30 75mm pack howitzer half-tracks, 81mm mortar half-tracks, M6 37mm gun motor carriages, M5 light tanks, and 2.5-ton trucks. On 29 December 1942 Captain Lennen led Company A and the French Infantry in an attack in the vicinity of Pichon, Tunisia, and was cited for bravery by French general Alphonse Juin, commander of friendly French forces in North Africa. Company A, 2nd Platoon, disembarked USS *Stone* and bivouacked at Bilda Airport south of Algiers. Heavy equipment (tanks) was loaded onto flatcars at Hussein Dey (Algiers) on 19 December 1942 and sent to Fériana, with the remaining wheeled vehicles following. The company was attached to the 16th French Regiment on 16 December and moved into positions at Fonndouk el Okbi. The company reported to Col. Maurice Condroyer of the French Algerian Division at Pichon along with the 601st Tank Destroyer (TD) Battalion.

U.S. military doctrine at the time theorized that the mission of a tank battalion was to support infantry, while that of a tank destroyer battalion was to defeat enemy tanks. Tank destroyer battalions were equipped with the M3 75mm gun motor carriage. On 29 December, Company A attacked enemy positions at La Sauvagère Hue el Assel near Pichon and advanced 3,000 yards into enemy territory, with a loss of about two hundred Afrika Korps infantry on the German side. Company A was supported by 1st Platoon, Company A of the 601st Tank Destroyer Battalion, fifty French infantry, and two French artillery batteries using French 75mm cannons. The 70th lost Tanks #7 and #13, two 2.5-ton trucks, and one T30 75mm pack howitzer half-track. Sgt. William S. Rainey and the pack howitzer crew were killed during this engagement. The graves of T/5 Cesar P. Osborne, Pvt. Russell J. Boucher, and Pvt. William M. George were later found, their bodies buried by the Germans. The Germans had placed their ID tags in a bottle on the graves with a note stating, "Here lie three valorous American panzer soldiers who fell on 29 December 1942."

T30 75mm howitzer motor carriages used by tank destroyer battalions and light tank battalions. U.S. ARMY

M5 light tank #6 of Company C. DIXON

On 5 January 1943, Company A and the French infantry were driven from Fonndouk el Okbi by a panzer force of thirty-two German tanks, but they recaptured the town two days later. Pvt. Jewell W. Hagwood was killed in action. His body was recovered from a tank at La Sauvagère and buried next to Captain Steel of Company A, 601st TD Battalion. On 20 January 1943 seven trucks were used as bait to draw out enemy tanks. German medium and heavy tanks attacked but were dealt with by the 70th, 601st TD Battalion, and 6-pounder British antitank guns. On 31 January 1943, Company A was reattached to the 1st Infantry Division under the command of Maj. Gen. Terry Allen, often called "Terrible Terry" because of his informal and combative demeanor. In February 1943, the Allied forces fell back as a result of a big push by Rommel's forces, with the Germans advancing toward Gafsa, Fériana, and Sbeitla. On 21 February, 2nd Platoon, Company A, engaged German forces (Mark IV tanks), destroying one enemy tank and killing several soldiers, with no casualties sustained by the company.

Knocked-out German Panzerkampfwagen IV (panzer IV). TAYNTON

On 22 February, Company A attached to Groupment Conne (commanded by Colonel Conne) under the 19th French Army Corps and was assigned to guard the town of Kesra. On 27 February, Company A was strafed by Spitfires with French insignia, attesting to the confusion typical at that time in the war. On 5 March, Company A, by now attached to the Constantine Division (Gen. Joseph Edouard Welvert commanding) with two French infantry companies, guarded the left flank of the 34th Infantry Division during a reconnaissance in force to Pichon. The 1st and 3rd Platoons came under heavy antitank fire but escaped to a small stand of woods to regroup. The unit returned to bivouac with no casualties.

On 11 March, Company A attacked the enemy in the Ousseltia Valley with Allied air cover. The 7th Moroccan Infantry (Goums), excellent mountain fighters, was on the right flank. The 1st and 2nd Platoons attacked north and southeast of the town, while the 3rd Platoon engaged the enemy on Hill 506 on the Kairouan Road. The 3rd Platoon was supported by three platoons of Churchill tanks. After the fighting subsided, enemy aircraft arrived and mistakenly bombed their own positions.

On 26 March, an attack was made with French infantry through the Ousseltia Valley toward Hill 446 and to high ground on the east side of the Great Sidi Bou Rhib and Sidi Bou Ker. The 1st Battalion of the 9th Regiment de Tirailleurs Algériens (RTA) with five Renault tanks participated in the assault, with the 74th Goums on the right flank and a battalion of Moroccan Infantry on the left. On 28 March, they attacked with a battalion of the 7th RTA from the Jelba farm near Ras Dahra to the southeast on the Maktar–Pichon Road. Lt. Frank Anderson led the column with three tanks, accompanied by five trucks of infantry and two towed 37mm antitank guns. The next day, the enemy counterattacked with nine tanks, but the line held. Lt. Stewart J. Williams commanded the T30 75mm pack howitzer motor carriage and attempted to make contact with the enemy, but was unsuccessful. Major Dow of the British Army arrived with a squadron of Churchill tanks. With these reinforcements, the company attacked east on the line of Pichon Road from De Zouqamara to Hill 480 at Djeb-banat el Yassiles. They reached their objective with no enemy contact.

On 31 March, Capt. Altee W. Wampler took command of Company A, relieving Capt. Ralph Lennen who was transferred to headquarters at Tlemcen, Algeria. Captain Wampler used deception to deter the Germans from extending any farther into the Company A sector. He ordered the company to drive around a winding mountain road several times, giving enemy observers a false impression that a large force was in the area, despite the fact that there were only fifteen tanks. Later it was learned through the Intelligence Section G-2 that the Germans thought an armored division was present.

Panzer IV Ausf. (Model) G of Kampfgruppe (combined-arms formation) Lueder knocked out at Beja, Tunisia. The 70th often encountered this type of tank. ROBERTS

On 6 April, Company A was relieved by the British 6th Armored Division and assigned to protect the left flank of the British armored unit. The tide of the war was turning, and the Germans were falling back. Numerous engagements resulted in more enemy soldiers surrendering. Allied aircraft began to dominate the skies, reducing artillery and aircraft attacks on the 70th. German forces increasingly destroyed their equipment before they surrendered. Rommel had been transferred back to Germany by Adolf Hitler lest he be captured, which would have been a significant propaganda defeat. Approximately seven thousand men of the Hermann Goering Division, composed of sixteen tanks and six half-tracks, surrendered to Company A.

The company moved to attack position on 8 April 1943, under enemy artillery fire, with the objective of Maison des L'eaw. They were halted by enemy minefields, which they cleared before taking their objective. They immediately received orders from French general Welvert to support an attack on La Sauvagère.

Company A attacked a road junction 9 miles northeast of Pichon in support of a French armored unit on 10 April. General Welvert was killed when his vehicle struck a landmine. Captain Wampler had reported to division headquarters, so Major Dow was in command during the attack on the east side of the mountains along the Ousseltia–Kairouan Road. A squadron of Churchill tanks accompanied Company A, along with a battery of British antiaircraft artillery, four batteries of French artillery, and a company of Goums in tanks. On 11 April, Company A was ordered to move to the next objective about twelve miles away through very difficult terrain. Three enemy antitank guns fired on three of the tanks, plus the command and staff tank, just short of the objective. Lieutenant Williams's and Lieutenant Anderson's tanks were hit and withdrew to what was thought to be a protected position, but the enemy opened up with mortar fire. The terrain was too rough for an effective tank attack, so a battalion of Goum infantry was brought up and successfully overran the enemy position.

Company A moved to bivouac positions north of Pichon on 12 April, performing maintenance and other administrative duties. On 25 April, Company A supported a unit of French Somua S35 tanks in a successful attack on Dj. Mansour, Tunisia. From 26 April to 6 May, Company A moved to various positions to protect flanks of attacking forces. On 7 May, Company A, attached to Groupment Blinde, moved to the El-Alaoui–Pont du Fahs road, traveling easterly through Pont du Fahs in an attempt to cut off the enemy retreat. Company A fell under artillery fire from 8 to 10 May, protecting flanks of Allied attacking forces and taking prisoners.

On 11 May, Company A moved to Huef Bou Zid in preparation to support and attack, beginning at 0930. Accompanying General Le Couteaux to Bir et Teila was 2nd Platoon. The units attacked positions at Bled Harabi. Captain Wampler and Lt. Frederick W. Boatwright with the 3rd Platoon and Lt. Stu Williams with the 2nd Platoon joined the attack. Over 1,500 Italian prisoners were taken, along with equipment and vehicles. On the attack against the town of Zaghouan, the Germans began destroying equipment, and the German commander, Colonel Becker, surrendered unconditionally to Lieutenant Williams. Apparently, among the Germans, the protocol for surrender was to first destroy weapons and have the German commander surrender to an Allied officer. Over 7,000 German soldiers surrendered. Prisoners were taken to the POW camp at Pont de Fahs. Company A made contact with the British Eighth Army on 13 May.

On 13 May 1943, Company A moved to attack positions in the vicinity of Heuncher Djeradou, but was overwhelmed by the surrender of thousands of German and Italian soldiers. They captured 210 enemy vehicles intact along with over 10,000 enemy prisoners. On 22 May, Company A was ordered back to Tlemcen to rejoin the battalion. This was essentially the end of the Africa campaign.

Bivouac area, Company B. DIXON

70th tanks lined up for inspection. TAYNTON

COMPANY B

On 7 November 1942, Company B landed at Safi under command of Lt. J. A. Wilson and was attached to 1st Battalion, 477th Infantry Regiment, 9th Division. The 2nd Platoon, commanded by Walter T. Anderson, was attached to 2nd Battalion, 47th Infantry Regiment. Tanks were lowered into lighters while the troops were transported ashore in Landing Craft Vehicle, Personnel (LCVP). Tank #1, commanded by Lieutenant Wilson, was the first 70th tank to land on the shores of North Africa. The tank crew consisted of Cpl. William H. Winter, Pvt. John Caputo, and Pvt. Paul Elinsky, who carried ashore the first American flag raised in North Africa. They landed at night without incident. The first objective was a French fort that turned on a searchlight to assess the situation. Immediately the battleship *New York* opened up with its 14-inch guns, and the searchlight went out. There was some small-arms fire upon landing, but French resistance was minimal, and the fort and town were consolidated quickly by the invasion force.

Company B was then ordered to Port Lyautey. They first passed through Casablanca, where the 1st and 2nd Platoons of Company B took part in a large parade with General Patton's 2nd Armored Division. It was not unusual for the Germans to refer to the 70th as the 70th Armored Division. After the parade, Company B continued to Port Lyautey and eventually joined Company C at the start of the new year to await the arrival of the rest of the battalion.

Moroccan cavalry, Casablanca, 1943. TAYNTON

French officers view parade, Casablanca, 1943. TAYNTON

USS *Susan B. Anthony* prior to landing. MCATEE

COMPANY C

On 8 November 1942 Company C landed at 0130 hours off Port Lyautey under covering fire from U.S. Navy escorts and attacks from shore batteries and French patrol boats. Six tanks from the USS *Henry T. Allen* and six tanks from the USS *Susan B. Anthony* came ashore along with one half-track and one jeep from the USS *Clymer*. During the landing, Sgt. Mason T. Wrenn, T/5 Harvey L. Ford, and Privates Elmer B. Hackworth and Aaron Schonman drowned. The company spent the day unloading vehicles and mopping up resistance. At 0800 on 9 November, Company C attacked an enemy armored position south of Mehdia, resulting in a rout of the enemy armor. Artillery fire was directed at the road in advance of the company to clear the way. Company C was then attached to the 1st Battalion, 60th Combat Team, but on the way to join them the company engaged two companies of enemy infantry who withdrew rapidly as a result of the firepower of the U.S. tanks. Toward the end of the day, Company C was subjected to enemy artillery fire as well as bombing by a U.S. Navy sea plane. On 10 November, Company C cleared out enemy machine-gun positions and antitank guns near Port Lyautey, demonstrating the U.S. Armored Corps doctrine of using tanks to oppose and defeat enemy infantry. Company C took up defensive positions outside the city at the airport, and hostilities ceased.

Company C, 70th Tank Battalion, in review for President Roosevelt, Morocco, January 1943. U.S. ARMY

President Roosevelt is seated in the jeep to the left, while Company C passes in review during a parade at the Casablanca Conference, January 1943. U.S. ARMY

On the morning of 11 November 1942, Capt. William A. Edwards led an attack by Company C and an infantry company, and captured the airdrome at Port Lyautey, taking many prisoners in the process. He was awarded the Silver Star by Brig. Gen. Lucian K. Truscott.

President Roosevelt attended the Casablanca Conference (14–24 January 1943) along with many dignitaries from the Allies to plan for future operations and celebrate the North African victories. During that time, Company C of the 70th participated in a celebration parade. Because of his disability from polio, the president sat in the front passenger seat of a jeep (see photo) rather than standing at attention to review the parade.

At the end of January 1943, Company C and an assault-gun detachment were sent to guard the Spanish–Moroccan border over concern that Gen. Francisco Franco, the new dictator of Spain and a German sympathizer, might send forces to attack the Americans. The mission of Company C was to keep an eye on border traffic and warn the 9th Infantry Division in Port Lyautey of any impending attack. Counter Intelligence Corps (CIC) personnel were active in the area and reported on Spanish troop movements across the border. After two weeks of duty, Company C was relieved and moved back to Port Lyautey.

SERVICE COMPANY

Service Company convoy on the trek from Casablanca to Tlemcen. An amphibious jeep (GPA) was the lead vehicle. DIXON

Service Company was a noncombat unit that supplied ammunition, food, and equipment, and performed repairs to vehicles. On 26 January 1943, Service Company personnel disembarked USS *Santa Rosa* and moved to the Lighthouse Camp south of Casablanca. General Marshall visited the camp at this time, having just attended the Casablanca Conference. More equipment was received from the ship on 28 January, and elements of the Service Company moved with the 70th Tank Battalion Headquarters Company to Port Lyautey just north of Rabat, the capital of French Morocco, on 28 January. Chief Warrant Officer Arrington B. Turner and Capt. Lewis C. Taynton remained at Casablanca as the battalion coordinated vehicle and equipment movements. Service Company reorganized, and on 5 February they consolidated equipment and boarded trains for the polo-field camp at Tlemcen, Algeria, where they arrived on 7 February. On 14 February, Captain Taynton became commander of Service Company, relieving Lieutenant O'Leary, who assumed command of the reconnaissance platoon. Captain Taynton lectured to his troops that he was the "hub and you are the spokes." From that point on, Captain Taynton was nicknamed "The Hub."

On 19 February, after enduring the weather in the mountains, including high winds, rain, and snow, Service Company moved with the battalion to Caserne Bedeau, Tlemcen, to an old Foreign Legion barracks, a much nicer camp. Service Company was assigned police duties in the town and continued to administer supplies and perform maintenance duties. During this period, the members of the 70th had the opportunity to attend church services at the Hotel des Voyageurs in Tlemcen. The troops who were sick as a result of being given Atebrin, an early preventative treatment for malaria, were able to recover at this time. On 23 March, French officers and enlisted men arrived for training in the M5 light tanks, which included operation instructions along with vehicular maintenance.

Throughout April and May, Service Company participated in routine duties. On 30 May, they moved with the battalion through Misserghin, La Senia, Sidi Chami, Assi-bou-Nif, St. Leu, and Port fe la Macta to a site near Debrousseville. The campsite was slightly less than desirable, and the men referred to it as "Mosquito Hill Camp." Many members of the battalion went swimming for the first time in the Mediterranean

Sea. In June, Service Company performed administrative activities, received new equipment, and performed maintenance. On 14 June, while they were in the area, the king of England and Generals Eisenhower, Patton, Bradley, and Clark reviewed Combat Team 39, an infantry regiment augmented by the 70th Tank Battalion, artillery units, and other combat units. It was under the command of the 9th Infantry Division and was a substantial attacking force.

By 30 June, Service Company loaded onto LSTs getting ready to invade Sicily, where they were to land with the other companies.

Customized tent. TAYNTON

BATTALION HEADQUARTERS

The battalion headquarters, minus advance elements, loaded onto USS *Santa Rosa* of the Grace Line at Staten Island Terminal, New York City, at 1130 hours on 13 January 1943. The ship's captain was Captain Rogers, and Major Hanchey was the permanent army officer on board. There were 2,500 troops and 125 officers on board from the air corps, tank destroyer units, infantry units, finance, medics, and tank units. The convoy was composed of the battleship *New York*, the cruiser *Brooklyn*, eight destroyers, eight troop transports, and ten cargo ships. Three days later, on 16 January 1943, the convoy was at north 37 degrees latitude, west 60 degrees longitude, and traveling at 15 knots, a relatively fast speed for a convoy.

USS *Santa Rosa.* U.S. NAVY

USS *Brooklyn* (CL40) light cruiser, commissioned 1937, escorting the fleet. TAYNTON

Troop transport accompanying the *Santa Rosa.* TAYNTON

In a 20 January 1943 memorandum from Capt. Michael C. Varhol, the transport commander on the *Santa Rosa*, members of the 70th were warned that leaving portholes open, smoking, or lighting matches on open decks would be considered a treasonable act that would subject offenders to punishment under the 75th Article of War. Water conservation was a problem as well, with so many troops crammed in quarters and a long voyage ahead. Strict rationing was enforced. The man-overboard procedure was explained to the troops: the men were cautioned to keep their feet off the rails when on deck. The ship would not stop for anyone falling overboard. An attempt would be made to rescue the individual while underway. If the rescue proved unsuccessful, the bridge would contact a trailing escort vessel to aid if possible.

Catholic Mass was held at 1100 hours each day, officiated by Chaplain Francis S. Spadaro, while Protestant services were held on Sundays at 1230 hours, officiated by Chaplain C. E. Mull. Special activities were established to relieve the boredom of the voyage. Captain Taynton was in charge of the band, quiz programs, and community singing. Lieutenants Geandrot and Corkill were in charge of musical recordings. Lieutenants Nicholas R. Corrado, Harold W. Miller, and Strickland directed recreation, and Lieutenant Caunt handled the library. Various units volunteered to entertain the men. Captain Taynton requested personnel with musical talent to report to him so that they could be included in the entertainment.

All soldiers were instructed to turn in their U.S. currency to the finance officer, Capt. William Tinsley, for "Special Military Currency," or military payment certificates (MPC). This policy was invoked to prevent problems associated with local currencies because of the desirability of the American dollar. (A large amount of American dollars injected into a foreign economy would make the local currency nearly worthless and encourage black markets.)

On board the *Santa Rosa*, Captain Varhol wrote a 23 January 1943 memorandum to all unit commanders indicating that the medical detachment would perform a physical examination of all troops the next day to verify the health of the troops, confirm that they were free from any contagious or infectious disease, eliminate those unable to travel with their units by virtue of any temporary or permanent disability, and ascertain the number of personnel requiring special treatment, including dentures and glasses. During the examination, the troops were to dress only in raincoats and shoes. Each unit was to have a roster from which men unfit for duty would be extracted and presented to the transport surgeon. Medical officers on duty on the *Santa Rosa* were Captain MacNeill (transport surgeon), Captain Baumgart, and Lieutenants Wisnefski, Harris, and Grant.

The following was to be read to all troops by commanders in advance of the examination:

> DOES ANY MAN KNOW OF ANY CONDITION WHICH IS LIKELY TO INTERFERE WITH HIS EFFICIENCY, SAFETY, OR HEALTH IN THE POSITION TO WHICH HE IS ASSIGNED? DOES ANY MEMBER OF THIS ORGANIZATION SUFFER FROM ANY OF THE FOLLOWING:
> Loss of weight not attributable to the voyage.
> Persistent cough, blood in the sputum, fever, or chills.
> Urethral discharge, penile sore, or known syphilis.
> Hernia, rupture, or abdominal pain on lifting.
> Eye strain, recurrent headaches, or need for glasses. (Specify)
> Tooth requiring filling, extraction or replacement of temporary filling. (Specify)
> Need for dental bridge or plate. (Specify number of teeth missing)
> Itching, cracking, or sores between the toes.
> Weakness, pain, deformity or other disease not mentioned above.

Daily bulletins provided a variety of information, such as leadership assignments to the troops. The daily bulletin on 17 January 1943 announced that the destination was French Morocco, subject to change. On 25 January, the *Santa Rosa* docked at Casablanca, French Morocco. There were several destroyed hulls of the French Navy, including the battleship *Jean Bart*. On 26 January, Headquarters Company moved to a bivouac north of the city near the lighthouse and set up the command post. General Patton visited the camp that day.

HEADQUARTERS U. S. S. SANTA ROSA
Office of the Transport Commander

January 13, 1943.

DAILY BULLETIN

1. GUARD:

Officer of the Day......................2nd Lt. Strickland, 1540-TT
Officer of the Guard....................2nd Lt. Koch, 5995-C

2. The names of permanent and temporary ship's personnel are listed below for the information and guidance of all concerned.

Permanent Personnel

Transport Commander...................Major H. W. Hantsche
Transport Surgeon.....................Captain MacNeill
Transport Chaplain (Protestant).......1st Lt. Mull

Temporary Assignments

Commanding Officer of Troops..........Lt. Col. J. C. Welborn
Transport Adjutant....................Captain M. C. Varhol
Prison Officer........................2nd Lt. F. E. Songer
Mess Officer..........................1st Lt. Irwin A. Hirsch
Recreation Officer....................2nd Lt. N. R. Corrado
Police & Sanitation Officer...........1st Lt. Harry Volk
Orchestra Leader......................Capt. L. C. Taynton
Chaplain (Catholic)...................Capt. Spadaro

3. MEALS: Meals will be served to officers and troops as follows:

Officers-- Begin Breakfast 0800
Begin Supper 1630

Troops---- Begin Breakfast 0700
Begin Supper 1500

(Enlisted Men will furnish their own Mess Gear)

Typical daily bulletin aboard ship informing the troops of leadership assignments. EISENHOWER PRESIDENTIAL LIBRARY

El Hank Light, Casablanca, French Morocco, North Africa. This was the location of the Lighthouse Camp on 26 January 1943. TAYNTON

Battalion officers at Casablanca. TAYNTON

Atlas Mountains, North Africa, on the way to Tlemcen, Algeria. TAYNTON

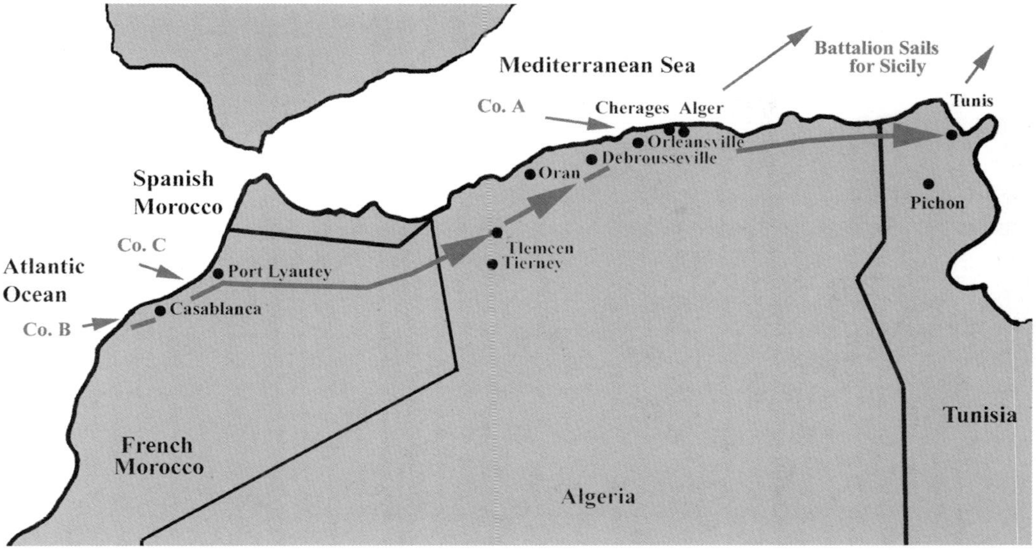

The location of the elements of the 70th as they fought through North Africa. ROBERTS

Caserne Bedeau, Tlemcen, was where the 70th command post was located from 19 February to 30 May 1943. DIXON

NORTH AFRICA

26 Jan/43	Lighthouse Camp	Casablanca, French Morocco N. Africa
29 Jan/43	Cork Grove Camp	Port Lyautey " " " "
7 Feb/43	Polo Field Camp	Tlemcen, Algeria, N. Africa
8 Feb/43	Snow Mountain Camp	Tierney, " " "
19 Feb/43	Cascerne Bedeau Camp	Tlemcen, " " "
30 May/43	Mosquito Hill Camp	DeBrousseville, Algeria, N. Africa
10 June/43	Airport Camp (Five miles east of Oran)	" "
15 June/43	Transient Camp	Orleansville " "
16 June/43	Staging Camp	Cherages " "
7 July/43	Aboard Marion S. Bouavc, Port of Algers	" "

70th camp locations in North Africa. TAYNTON

On 29 January, the command post was moved to Port Lyautey (the Cork Forest), reuniting it with units from B and C Companies. Captain Taynton, Warrant Officer Turner, and other men remained in Casablanca to supervise the unloading of equipment and arranging transportation to 70th units. On 4 February 1943, the 70th was ordered to Tlemcen via train and convoy through the Atlas Mountain range that crossed the northwestern and north-central portions of North Africa.

TLEMCEN

Upon arriving in Algeria, the 70th bivouacked at the racetrack in Tlemcen on 8 February, moving shortly afterward to Tierney, Algeria, where they set up tents in sleet and snowy weather on a hillside just south of town. The headquarters moved to Caserne Bedeau on 19 February. The 70th was detached from the 9th Division and attached to Fifth Army headquarters. The mission was to train French officers on the M5 light tank, run the railroad operations in the area, and administer the hospital. Lieutenant Colonel Welborn was in charge of the town while Captain Varhol was the provost martial. Under the Fifth Army, the 70th was attached to VI Corps with the code name "Raincoat." Garrison duty included policing the town, operating the camp, and guarding strategic locations. When on leave in town, there were three approved bars (Chez Pepico, La Belle Rose, and La Favorite) along with a French movie house.

Service Club, Tlemcen. TAYNTON

Place de l'indépendance, Tlemcen. TAYNTON

Minaret de Mansourah, Tlemcen. TAYNTON

On 19 February 1943, the 70th was detached from the 9th Infantry Division. According to 9th intelligence, no enemy ground forces remained in Algeria, with the westernmost Axis line being approximately a hundred and fifty miles east of Constantine, Algeria. Axis forces in Tunisia were estimated at 180,000 with a number of tanks and aircraft. Allied forces had engaged Rommel about seventy-five miles west of Sfax, Tunisia. The town of Gafsa was taken by the enemy. Enemy aircraft were active along the Algerian coast and Algerian–Tunisian boarder. German saboteurs had been landing by glider in Algeria in an attempt to disrupt Allied operations.

Bus stop, Tlemcen. TAYNTON

Place de l'Indépendance, Tlemcen. TAYNTON

From left to right, standing: Capt. Donald Flessa, Lt. Edward Jones (fourth from left), Captain Taynton (fifth from left), Lt. Gordon Brodie (sixth from left), Capt. Michael Varhol (seventh from left), Capitaine Pinion (third from right, French officer), Lieutenant Colonel Welborn (second from right), and Capt. Joseph Wisnefski. Kneeling on the left is Lt. John Ahern. In the background is a Dodge WC56 command car. Photo taken at Caserne Bedeau, Tlemcen, February 1943. DIXON

Captain Taynton in front of a T2 tank retriever. Note the pipe in the upper turret, which is a fake gun. Since the primary mission of the T2 was to recover disabled tanks, it was considered unnecessary to have guns mounted on the vehicle; consequently, all guns were fake. T2 commanders took orders from battalion headquarters only. TAYNTON

Captain Bushey. TAYNTON

Captain Varhol, Maj. Henry E. Davidson, and Lieutenant Colonel Welborn in Algeria, 1943. ERICKSON

Special services movie location, probably at the Mosquito Camp. ERICKSON

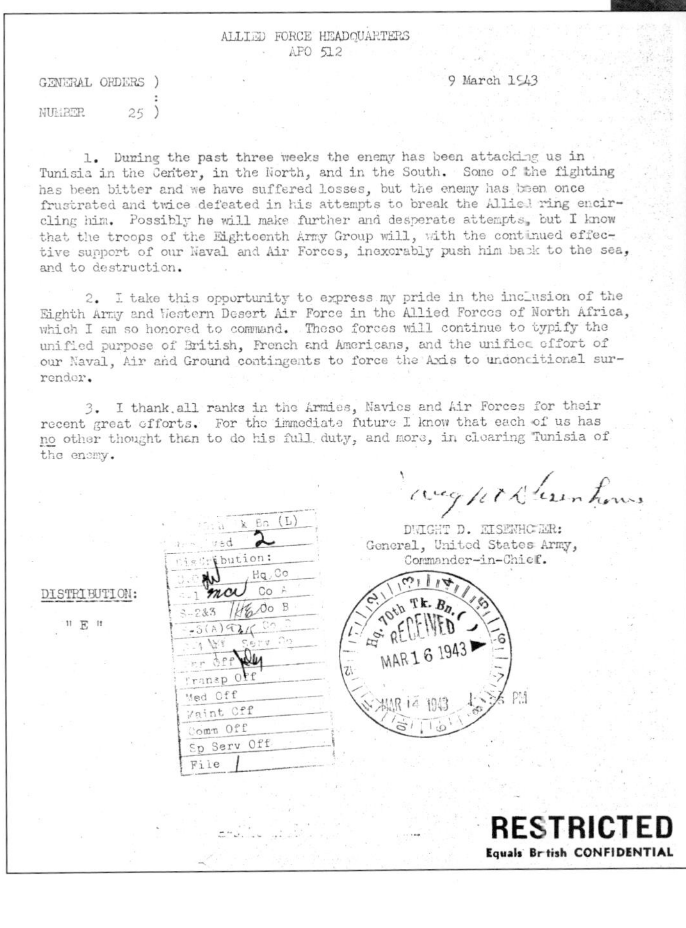

ALLIED FORCE HEADQUARTERS
APO 512

GENERAL ORDERS)
:
NUMBER 25)

9 March 1943

1. During the past three weeks the enemy has been attacking us in Tunisia in the Center, in the North, and in the South. Some of the fighting has been bitter and we have suffered losses, but the enemy has been once frustrated and twice defeated in his attempts to break the Allied ring encircling him. Possibly he will make further and desperate attempts, but I know that the troops of the Eighteenth Army Group will, with the continued effective support of our Naval and Air Forces, inexorably push him back to the sea, and to destruction.

2. I take this opportunity to express my pride in the inclusion of the Eighth Army and Western Desert Air Force in the Allied Forces of North Africa, which I am so honored to command. These forces will continue to typify the unified purpose of British, French and Americans, and the unified effort of our Naval, Air and Ground contingents to force the Axis to unconditional surrender.

3. I thank all ranks in the Armies, Navies and Air Forces for their recent great efforts. For the immediate future I know that each of us has <u>no</u> other thought than to do his full duty, and more, in clearing Tunisia of the enemy.

DWIGHT D. EISENHOWER:
General, United States Army,
Commander-in-Chief.

DISTRIBUTION:
" E "

RESTRICTED
Equals British CONFIDENTIAL

Memorandum from General Eisenhower that came across the 70th HQ desk, thanking all units for the efforts in the campaign. NATIONAL ARCHIVES

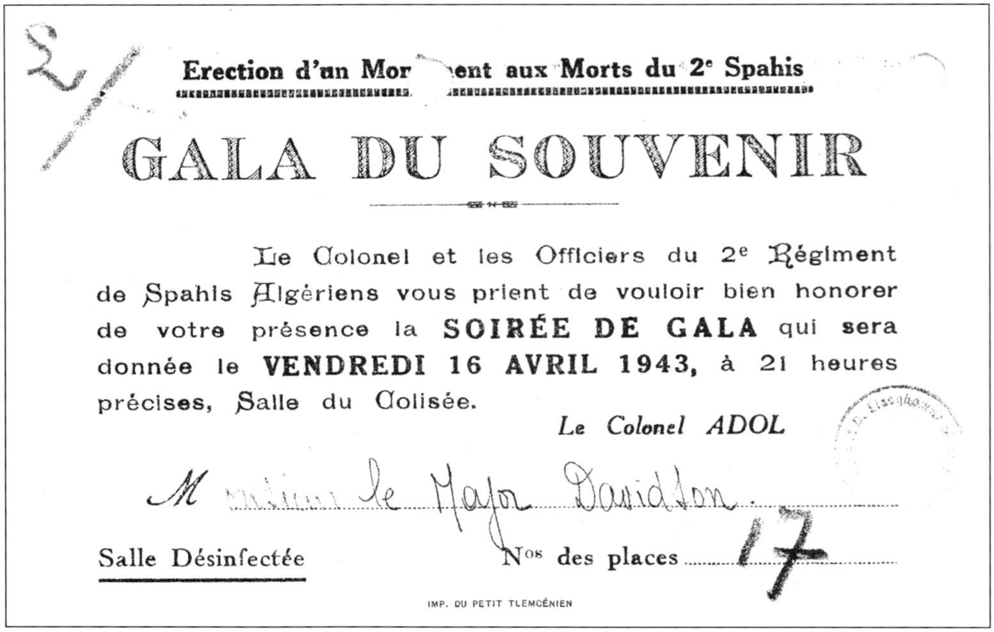

2/

Erection d'un Mor[illegible]ent aux Morts du 2e Spahis

GALA DU SOUVENIR

Le Colonel et les Officiers du 2e Régiment de Spahis Algériens vous prient de vouloir bien honorer de votre présence la **SOIRÉE DE GALA** qui sera donnée le **VENDREDI 16 AVRIL 1943**, à 21 heures précises, Salle du Colisée.

Le Colonel ADOL

M onsieur le Major Davidson

Salle Désinfectée — Nos des places 17

IMP. DU PETIT TLEMCÉNIEN

The 70th officers received many invitations to attend various events in North Africa. Lieutenant Colonel Welborn received so many invitations from the French and local government officials that he decided to decline all of them, lest he offend someone. This invitation to attend a dedication of a monument to those deceased from the 2nd Spahis unit is addressed to Major Davidson from Colonel Adol. EISENHOWER PRESIDENTIAL LIBRARY

Captured enemy vehicle converted for Allied use. This appears to be a Fiat Type 508 light utility vehicle, 32-horsepower engine with top speed of 50 miles per hour. This vehicle was commonly used by the Italian Army. DIXON

At the end of March, several classes of French squads arrived for a two-week school in M5 light tank operation. The first week involved learning about the tanks, the principles of operation, and theory. The second week involved practical exercises at the firing range on the south side of the Atlas Mountains near Sebdou. Capitaine Pinon, liaison between the French and American units, provided translation.

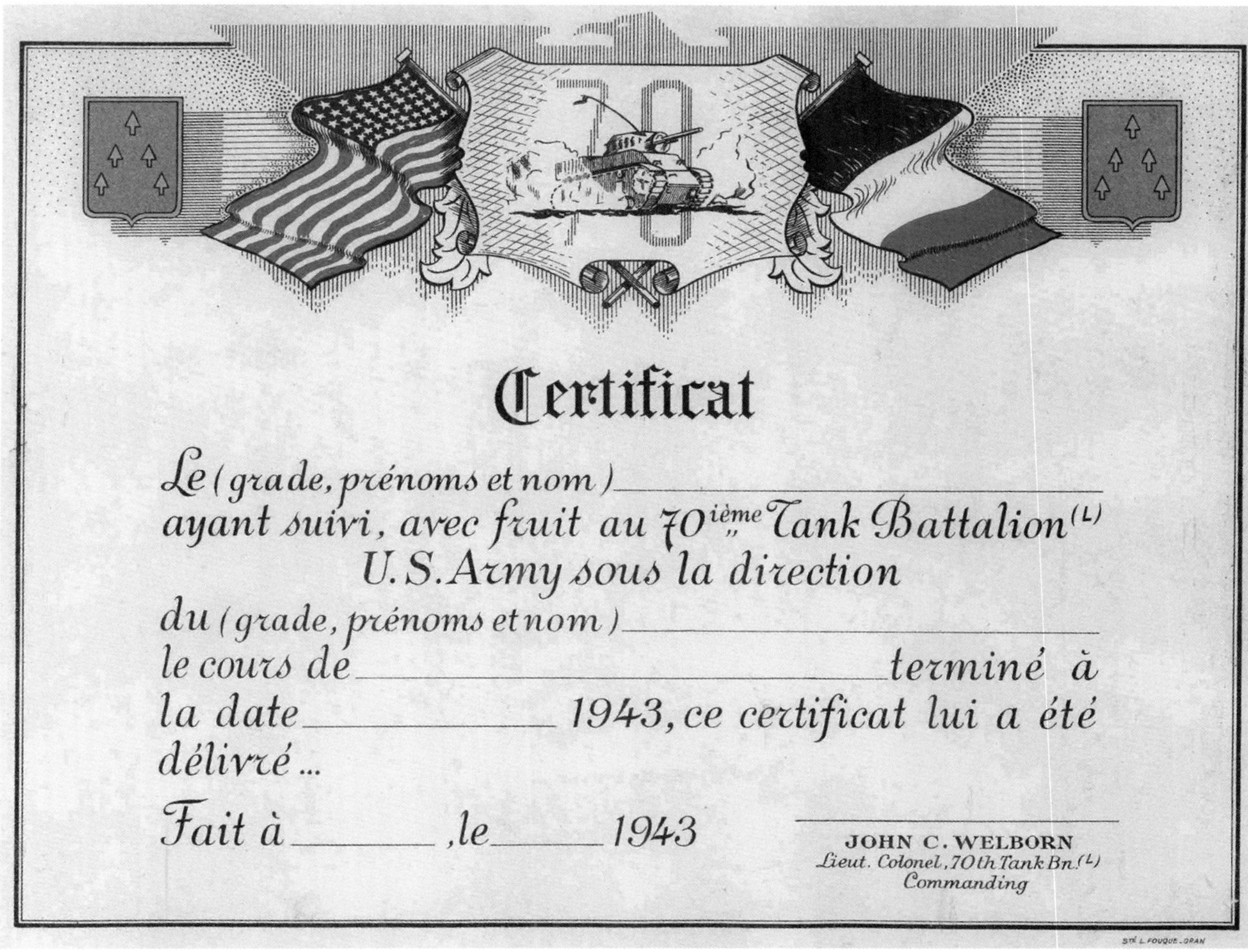

Certificat

Le (grade, prénoms et nom) ________
ayant suivi, avec fruit au 70ième Tank Battalion (L)
U.S. Army sous la direction
du (grade, prénoms et nom) ________
le cours de ________ terminé à
la date ________ 1943, ce certificat lui a été
délivré...

Fait à ______ , le ______ 1943

JOHN C. WELBORN
Lieut. Colonel, 70th Tank Bn. (L)
Commanding

When the French switched loyalty from the Vichy government to the Allies, the 70th was charged with training their units on operating the M5 light tanks. At the end of each course the French tankers received the above certificate. TAYNTON

PREPARATION FOR INVASION OF SICILY

On 30 May 1943, the 70th was moved under secret orders to Arzew, Algeria. With enemy forces having been cleared from Tunisia, Company A arrived and joined the 70th at "Mosquito Hill." Company A had just completed an extensive Tunisian campaign supporting French forces. The 70th was attached to the 1st Infantry Division and preparations were made for an amphibious landing at an unknown shore. The 70th then moved to the high ground near Chéraga and prepared for amphibious operations with protective shrouds mounted on the M5 light tanks. On 6 July 1943, the 70th boarded the USS *Mexico* on the way to Sicily.

Destroyed town in North Africa. TAYNTON

Photo of a rare M6 37mm gun motor carriage. These vehicles were declared obsolete after the North African campaign and most were recycled or given to the Marine Corps. TAYNTON

Panzer III Ausf. N, 2nd Company, 501st Heavy Panzer Battalion, Tunisia, 1943. ROBERTS

Panzer IV Ausf. G, Kampfgruppe Lueder, lost during Operation Ochsenkopf at Beja, Tunisia, 1943. ROBERTS

Panzer III Ausf. L, 2nd Company, Heavy Tank Battalion 501 of Kampfgruppe Lueder lost during Operation Ochsenkopf at Beja, Tunisia, 1943. ROBERTS

Panzer III Ausf. L, Tunisia, 1943. ROBERTS

Panzer VI "Tiger" 121 of 1st Company, Heavy Tank Battalion 504, Tunisia, 1943. The protective recoil mechanism sleeve has been dislodged, possibly as a result of battle damage. This was a formidable weapon and feared by tankers on the battlefield. ROBERTS

Panzer VI "Tiger" 231 of 2nd Company, Heavy Tank Battalion 501, knocked out on the Robaa Road, Tunisia, 1943. ERICKSON

From left to right: Lieutenant Colonel Welborn, commanding officer; Major Davidson, executive officer; and Captain Varhol, adjutant. June 1943, Cheragas, Algeria. U.S. ARMY

Sebdou, March 17, 1943

To the Administrator
Commune mixte de SEBDOU

I have the honor to inform you that an American military truck, on the 12 inst., towards 0800 AM, collided with my mare and caused its death.

Circumstances were as follows:

I was on horseback holding the mare that followed with a rein - Some American military light trucks overpassed me, and my two animals kept quiet - But another American truck belonging to the same convoy came a little later, my mare then took fear and backed up. I was unable to manage it and hoping it would take to the fields, I let it go. But the truck running too fast, it was too late, and the mare was struck behind. As the driver did not try to slow down, the collision was violent.

Certainly, I am partly to blame for what happened, but is is sure that had the chauffeur slackened the speed of the car, the accident could not have taken place.

My mare was aged 8 years and was bought for 8000 francs.

As a poor native living on very meagre resources, I beg of you to forward this claim to the proper authority and do what you can about it so that I be indemnified for the loss of my mare.

This document, received at the 70th headquarters, is a claim for loss of property caused by U.S. Army trucks. It alleges that a 70th Tank Battalion truck struck and killed a horse owned by the claimant, who begged for compensation. EISENHOWER PRESIDENTIAL LIBRARY

CHAPTER 3

Operation Husky: The Invasion of Sicily

THE LANDING

The Operation Husky battle plan called for landing the British Eighth Army (Montgomery) near Syracuse and the Seventh Army (Patton), of which the 70th was part, near Gela. The 70th was together for the first time since debarkation from the United States, and was attached to the 1st Infantry Division, the "Big Red One." An advance party commanded by Captain Wampler on 10 July 1943 acted as a guide for the rest of the battalion that landed between 13 and 15 July. The battalion staff and thirty-five enlisted men landed at Gela on 13 July and proceeded on Highway 115 out of the city. The battalion continued along a winding road through war debris consisting of burned vehicles, landing craft, and supplies to the bivouac 4 miles north of Gela. There was considerable activity on the beach where landing craft shuttled supplies, equipment, and munitions. From 14 to 15 July the tanks came ashore, fording kits were removed, and the tanks were made ready for battle. The battalion strength was forty-five tanks, three assault guns (T30 75mm howitzer motor carriage), three mortar half-tracks, and other assorted half-tracks.

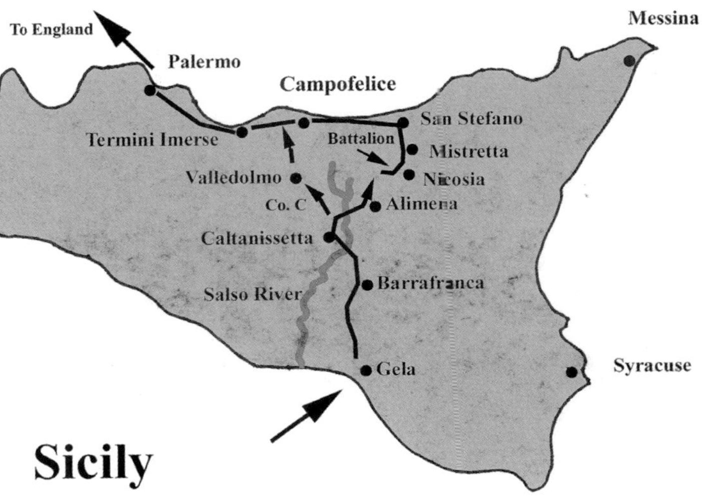

Map of Sicily. ROBERTS

BARRAFRANCA

For the first time as a complete battalion, the 70th was ordered to secure the high ground northeast of Barrafranca, supporting the 26th Infantry Regiment. The M5 light tanks and T30 75mm pack howitzer motor carriages were used in the attack, which started on the morning of 16 July. Companies B and C were in a flank formation, with Company A in reserve with the assault-gun platoon in support. As the flank advanced, the 70th was forced to use the roads because the terrain was not suitable for tanks. The Germans opened up on the road, having zeroed in their weapons prior to the attack. The troops withdrew to the jumping-off point, which was immediately attacked by sixteen German panzer IV tanks that were not supposed to be in the vicinity, according to G-2. Lieutenant Colonel Welborn immediately withdrew the 70th tanks to high ground surrounding the road and directed fire with the 37mm guns onto the lightly armored tops of the German tanks, knocking out five of them and halting the attack. That afternoon, they resumed the attack on Barrafranca. The road had been mined, causing tanks to detour off road, a difficult task due to the terrain. About an hour after starting the second attack, they captured and secured the town. The 26th Infantry Regiment occupied Barrafranca, while the 70th moved to the bivouac area nearby.

City of Gela, Sicily, 1943. TAYNTON

A photo of a rare M6 gun motor carriage equipped with a 37mm gun, the same gun on the tanks used by the 70th. This vehicle was found to be ineffective against German armor and declared obsolete shortly after it was deployed; it is unusual to see one in operation in Sicily. The soldiers seen here are rounding up fresh meat in Sicily, 1943. TAYNTON

German tanks knocked out in Sicily. The 70th pioneered tactics on this type of tank by ascending a hill, shooting down on the lightly armored top of the enemy tank, and then disappearing before the enemy tank could return fire. The top photo is of a Panzer III Ausf. M, while the bottom photo is of a Panzer III Ausf. L. TAYNTCN

M5 light tanks and an M6 gun motor carriage (second from right) used by the 70th. The 70th was not equipped with Sherman tanks until they redeployed to England. TAYNTON

The 70th started the battle with forty-five M5 light tanks, three assault-gun half-tracks, and three mortar half-tracks. Two tanks were destroyed and eight disabled. One half-track lost its track but was able to drive back on the front-wheel drive, rolling on the road wheels.

Orders were received from Gen. Theodore Roosevelt Jr., 1st Infantry Division, to capture the high ground north of Barrafranca on 17 July. Medium tanks were attached to the 70th from the 753rd Tank Battalion. The terrain was rocky and mountainous, forcing the tanks to take a winding road that the Germans easily defended. As enemy artillery zeroed in, the tanks took off at full speed, hatches closed, firing at the enemy while running the gauntlet and seizing the objective in the early morning. Companies B and C held the objective with the supporting infantry while the rest of the battalion was held in reserve. The enemy hastily evacuated the area.

Company C (Lt. DeWitt C. Fair commanding) reconnoitered the Pietraperzia–Barrafranca road and ran into an extensive minefield. This caused the tanks to detour, exposing them to antitank fire registered in on these routes. The lead tank was hit and rolled over into a ditch. All the crew were evacuated, including Sgt. Paul J. Kovacik, Cpl. Elwood J. Silva, Pvt. Vincent S. DeVita, and Cpl. James B. Roberts. Company C withdrew to the high ground overlooking the Salso River and was attached to the 45th Infantry Division one mile south of Pietraperzia. Company A relieved Company C at the observation point near the Salso River. During the action from 16 to 17 July, the battalion lost one enlisted man, three wounded, and one tank destroyed, and took many German and Italian prisoners. On the seventeenth, General Roosevelt was conferring with officers at the 70th command post when an air attack ensued. Everyone hit the dirt before running to a cave nearby. Lt. Irwin A. Hirsch got there first, but stepped aside to let the general through. The general spoke up and said, "Go ahead, Lieutenant, there is no rank in a situation like this."

On 18 July, Company B led an attack across the Salso River along Highway 122 to Highway 117, to protect the right flank of the 1st Division. Company A was to attack toward Caltanissetta and Villarosa, but was thwarted by observer-directed artillery fire and retreated to defensive positions.

SALSO RIVER CROSSING

Company B forded the Salso River after the enemy had destroyed the bridge, and attacked enemy positions in that area. The dry terrain worked to the advantage of the 70th. They ignited dry wheatfields, and the smoke drove the enemy from their concealed positions. Toward evening hours, the 70th consolidated positions just northeast of the Salso. Company C, attached to the 45th Infantry Division, encountered tank and artillery resistance on the way to Pietraperzia. They captured enemy positions and turned over German and Italian prisoners to the infantry. Company C assaulted the town of Caltanissetta on 17 July with the aid of air support and the 45th.

The next two days involved a big push through Vallelunga Pratameno on Highway 121, where they captured equipment and many enemy prisoners. On 19 July, a patrol was sent out to investigate enemy activity on the mountain slope about two miles to the north. The patrol was hammered by machine-gun fire and Sgt. Hendrick A. Wansink was killed. The assault-gun and mortar sections were brought up and fired on the enemy position, igniting brush and setting the whole side of the mountain ablaze.

The Allied Air Force had finally gained superiority in the air and was pounding enemy positions. Observation aircraft such as the L4 (Piper Cub) called in accurate artillery fire on enemy positions. On 21 July, Company C destroyed six enemy light tanks in an attack toward Valledolmo north of Vallelunga. They overran the city of Collessano on 24 July, with the 1st Platoon continuing on to Campofelice. The 1st and 2nd Platoons attacked at Castelbuono. The 70th lost seven tanks, one half-track, and one officer and ten enlisted men wounded in the Salso River battle.

Captured Italian Semovente 90/53 self-propelled artillery, Sicily, 1943. TAYNTON

Italian Carro Comando on a knocked-out M13/40 Series III chassis, Sicily, 1943. TAYNTON

On 20 July, the 70th attacked and took Enna, with Company B taking the lead. Then the battalion attacked northwest to Villapriolo to link up with the 26th Infantry. They reached the Morello River but could not cross as the enemy had blown the bridges. The following day, B Company led an attack on Alimena supported by 36th Infantry Artillery units, the 26th Infantry Regiment, the 1st Engineering Battalion, and Company A 753 Medium Tank Battalion. The town fell, and the force moved on Bompietro the following morning, a town that was heavily defended. Antitank guns and an enemy counterattack slowed the advance. During the pitched battle, artillery was brought up in support and 70th tanks entered the town. Companies A and B took up positions just outside the town to ward off counterattacks by the Germans. The 26th Infantry took a beating while rooting out machine-gun nests and enemy infantry. During this action, five tanks were disabled, seven tankers killed, and five tankers wounded. The 70th withdrew to the area around Alimena to refuel, rearm, and rest.

SICILY

14 July/43	Olive Grove Camp	Gela, Sicily
16 July/43	Dawn Attack Camp	Barafranca, Sicily
17 July/43	Fox hole hill	Pie Traperzia, Sicily
18 July/43	Barons Camp	Near Caltanissette, Sicily
20 July/43	Lufty Heights Camp	20 Miles North of Caltanissette, Sicily
22 July/43	Camp Flessa, Alimena	Alimena, Sicily
25 July/43	Cannon Camp	Petralia, Sicily
26 July/43	Hay Field Camp	3 Miles North of Petralia, Sicily
27 July/43	Mountain Strong hold Camp	Gangi, Sicily
29 July/43	Long Tom Camp	Sperlinga, Sicily
30 July/43	Camp Mt. Etna	Nicosia, Sicily
1 Aug/43	Foggy Mountain Camp,	Mistretta, Sicily
26 Aug/43	Ocean View Camp	Termini-Imerese, Sicily
5 Nov/43	Staging Area Camp, Lido Mondello,	Palermo, Sicily
11 Nov/43	Aboard U.S.S. Monterey	Palermo Harbor, Sicily

70th Camps in Sicily. TAYNTON

PaK 38 German antitank gun (50mm). This gun was very effective and often encountered by the 70th. TAYNTON

On 22 July, the 70th was ordered to enter enemy territory and secure two bridges over the Acqua Amara River and hold until infantry arrived. This was dangerous, as there would be no infantry protection against enemy infantry-borne antitank weapons. Company B led the attack and, despite severe close-in combat, they took the objective by evening. The Germans were using "sticky bombs," grenades with an adhesive that allowed infantry to attach it to the hull of a tank.

In the previous thirteen days, the 70th had moved from the Sicilian south coast at Gela to almost the north coast, through mountainous terrain. The enemy was retreating rapidly toward Messina, the last exit to Italy. On 1 August, the 70th moved to bivouac on a mountain about three miles south of Mistretta under occasional attacks by enemy aircraft. Company C was back with the battalion after a stint with the 45th Infantry Division.

THE SICILY CAMPAIGN ENDS

The 70th was not involved in any more combat operations in Sicily after 1 August 1943 because the Germans had retreated to Italy across the Strait of Messina. The battalion entered a period of relaxation, training, gunnery practice, and typical camp duties. Tankers performed long-needed vehicle maintenance, and they were even able to view their first movie in months. The battalion cooks made deals with local farmers, and fresh meat and vegetables were available, which was a great improvement over C-rations.

On 26 August, the battalion moved to a camp location just east of Termini Imerese, where they underwent extensive gunnery and tank-operation training through November. Palermo was a popular nearby destination for the tankers. The Italians considered the Americans to be liberators and treated them very well. The tankers of the 70th obtained local building materials and constructed rather elaborate living quarters compared to their standard-issue tents. Intramural sport contests between companies ensued, including volleyball, football, and softball games, as well as track meets and games of horseshoes. The troops were ordered not to fire on enemy aircraft as they were probably landing at the nearby airport to surrender. On 5 November, the battalion moved to a staging area west of Palermo and boarded the USS *Monterey*, destination England.

Damaged bridge, Sicily, 1943. TAYNTON

Recon unit of the 70th, Sicily, 1943. TAYNTON

On 3 August 1943, Gen. George S. Patton slapped Pvt. Charles Kuhl, who was suffering from battle fatigue. This condition was not understood well at the time, and Patton considered such an affliction cowardly. This memo was received by the battalion from Patton, ordering that any soldier complaining of being "nervously incapable of combat" should be severely disciplined and sent to the front lines. This episode was highly publicized and nearly ended the general's career. The Germans were in disbelief that a skilled general would be fired for slapping a mere soldier. EISENHOWER PRESIDENTIAL LIBRARY

HEADQUARTERS SEVENTH ARMY
A. P. O. #758, U. S. ARMY

5 August 1943

MEMORANDUM:

TO : Corps, Division and Separate Brigade Commanders.

It has come to my attention that a very small number of soldiers are going to the hospital on the pretext that they are nervously incapable of combat. Such men are cowards, and bring discredit on the Army and disgrace to their comrades who they heartlessly leave to endure the danger of a battle which they themselves use the hospital as a means of escaping.

You will take measures to see that such cases are not sent to the hospital, but are dealt with in their units.

Those who are not willing to fight will be tried by Court-Martial for cowardice in the face of the enemy.

/s/ G. S. PATTON, JR.,
G. S. PATTON, JR.,
Lieutenant General, U.S. Army,
Commanding.

AG 250.1 (AG) 1st Ind. FWZ/wk
HQ II CORPS, APO 302, US Army, 7 August 1943.

To: Brigade and Separate Unit Commanders, II Corps.

For compliance by all commanders.

By command of Lieutenant General BRADLEY:

F. W. Zies.
F. W. ZIES,
Lt Col, A.G.D.,
Adjutant General.

DIST:
"B-1 less divisions"

Bivouac area near Palermo in August 1943. TAYNTON

Chow line at bivouac outside Palermo, 1943. TAYNTON

Dead German soldier (note hobnail boot sole) at a machine-gun position, Sicily, 1943. TAYNTON

British soldier, Sicily, 1943. TAYNTON

Lieutenant Taynton gets a haircut, Sicily, 1943. TAYNTON

Typical headquarters company M2 half-track, Sicily, 1943. TAYNTON

T2 tank-recovery vehicles constructed from obsolete M3 medium tanks, Sicily, 1943. TAYNTON

Recon platoon in Sicily, 1943. Back row (left to right): Lt. Carl Seeley, John Fritz, Ed Kosmalski, unknown, George Fuller, Leon J. Witkowski, Joseph J. Wisniewski, unknown. Second row: DeDona (fourth from left) and Sgt. Lewis H. Pollard (sixth from left). FRITZ

Recon jeeps at camp, Sicily, 1943. Note the field-modified jeep with .50-caliber machine-gun mount and tripwire protectors (poles) on the front to prevent decapitation. TAYNTON

Pistol practice as part of the training the 70th received after hostilities wound down in the fall of 1943. TAYNTON

This commandeered enemy vehicle appears to be a Fiat Type 508, the most widely used Italian utility vehicle. TAYNTON

Aircraft contrails. This appears to be bombers in formation attacking targets in Europe. Note the straight contrails of the bombers, while the curved contrails are likely fighter escorts that are much faster and must zigzag in order to stay with the bombers. TAYNTON

Recon jeep in Sicily, 1943. On the far left is Leon Witkowski. John Fritz is at the far right. FRITZ

Sergeant Tomasheski inspecting a German 7.5cm PaK 97/38 antitank gun, Sicily, September 1943. The lettering on the armored plate he is pointing to reads "Höchstgeschwindigkeit 20 km/std" ("maximum speed 20 km/hr"). TOMASHESKI

Anthony Kunitsky (left) and T/4 Francis Ross, Palermo, Sicily, 1943. ROSS

From left to right: John Fritz, L. C. Sproles, and Sam Mitchel on pass in Palermo, Sicily, 1943. FRITZ

Staging area outside Palermo. TAYNTON

T/5 Ross in Palermo, Sicily. ROSS

T/5 Ross (left) and Earl Daniels, Palermo, Sicily. ROSS

Captain Bushey, Sicily, 1943. TAYNTON

Cooks of the 70th, Sicily, 1943. TAYNTON

Lieutenant Corrado, S cily, 1943. TAYNTON

Lieutenant Hirsch, Sicily, 1943. TAYNTON

Captain Varhol, Sicily, 1943. TAYNTON

Captain Taynton near a sign pointing toward Messina where the Germans escaped to Italy. TAYNTON

Company C light tank with Captain Taynton and army nurses, Sicily, 1943. TAYNTON

Captain Wampler, Major Davidson, and Lieutenant Colonel Welborn, Sicily, 1943. TAYNTON

When the 70th became detached from the 1st Infantry Division, this letter of appreciation was received from Gen. Terry Allen, commanding general of the 1st. EISENHOWER MUSEUM

HEADQUARTERS 1ST US INFANTRY DIVISION
A.P.O. #1, U. S. ARMY

5 August 1943

TO: Commanding Officer, 70th Tk Bn (Lt).

Upon your relief from attachment to the Division and on passing from our direct control, I wish to thank you personally and in the name of the 1st US Infantry Division for the loyal cooperation of the 70th Tk Bn (Lt) during the Sicilian Campaign. The actions of the Bn at BARRAFRANCA, E of CALTANISSETTA, at ENNA, at ALIMENA and at BUON-PIETRO were fine examples of the intimate relationship that existed between the Division and your Battalion. They were also a tribute to your leadership, and to the courage and combat efficiency of your men, without whose assistance our common task would have been infinitely more difficult.

With every good wish for the future and the hope that you will again be with us when the going is tough, I remain

Most Sincerely,

Terry Allen

TERRY ALLEN
Major General, U.S. Army
Commanding.

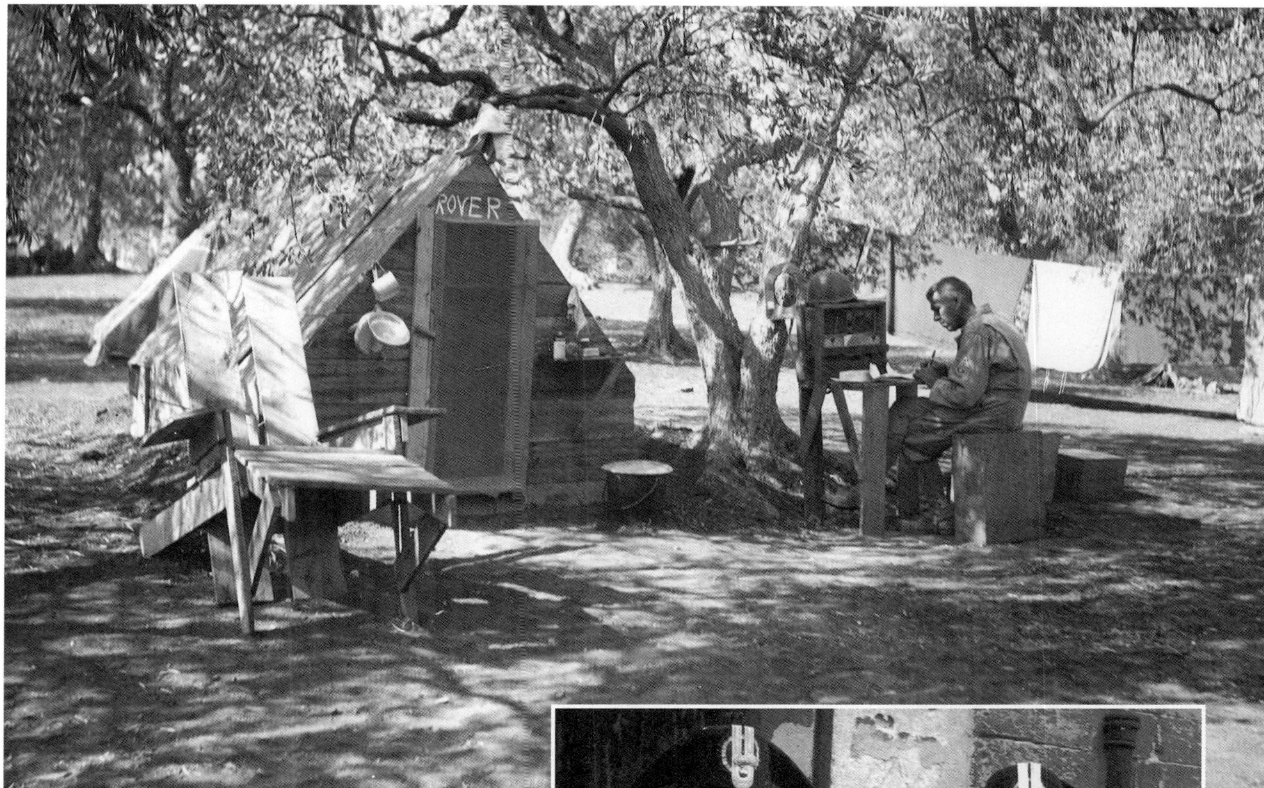

Sgt. Timmons W. Vassey performing paperwork in Service Company. After hostilities ceased in Sicily, the 70th had time to set up camp and obtain building materials to make this comparatively comfortable shelter. TAYNTON

Carabinieri, the national military police of Italy, 1943. TAYNTON

16

CHAPTER 4

England

MOVING TO SOUTHERN ENGLAND

The 70th boarded the USS *Monterey* in Sicily and sailed to England around the western side of Ireland, down the coast of Scotland, and through the Irish Sea to Liverpool. Convoy protection and the circuitous route were required because German submarines were based nearby off the coast of France. Although the troops had much more space aboard the *Monterey* than other ships, the usual monotony of sea voyages set in.

The *Monterey* arrived at low tide on 28 November 1943, but had to wait for the next favorable tide to make it into the docking facilities. Several other ships were competing for docking space as a result of the huge military buildup in England. The 70th arrived at the dock at about 2015 hours and the men quickly disembarked to trains that would take them to their new station, Ogbourne St. George, a British military camp near Swindon in the south of England. They encountered several Red Cross Clubmobiles (coffee and donut buses) on the way, welcome treats for the tankers of the 70th. After boarding a train for a short trip, the battalion arrived at Ogbourne St. George. Bags of mail were waiting, and a barber shop was set up to make the men presentable for passes to the nearby town of Swindon.

Red Cross Clubmobile (donut bus), England, 1943. TAYNTON

Red Cross Clubmobile, England, 1943. TAYNTON

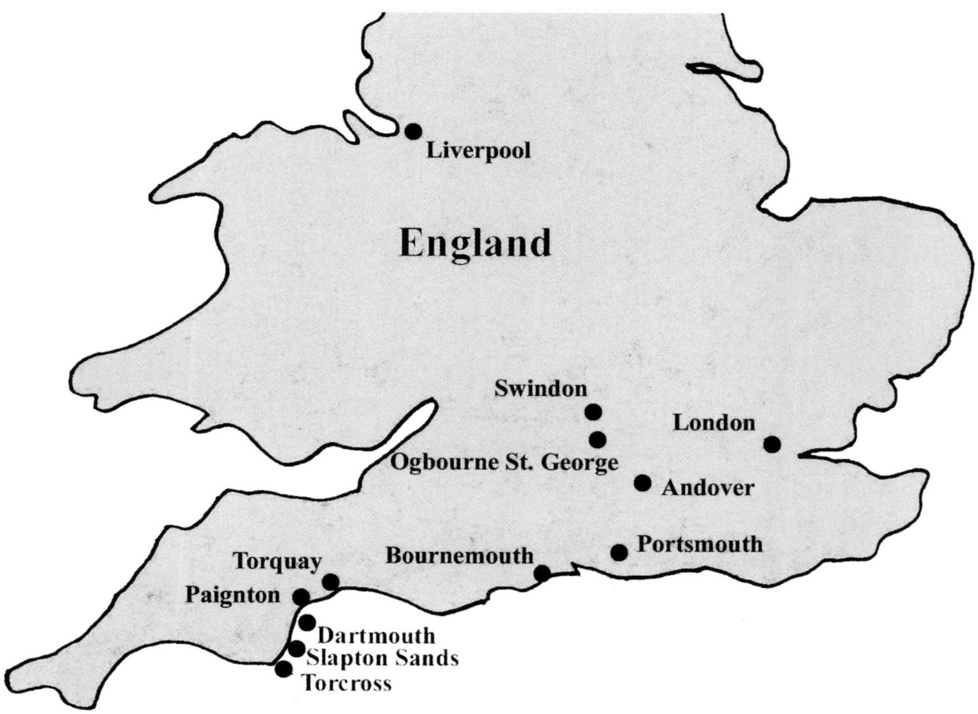

Various areas in England visited by 70th personnel. ROBERTS

A " short snorter," or dollar bill signed by several members of the 70th. Upon entry into a bar, a soldier could be challenged to show his "short snorter." If he could not produce it, he had to buy a round of drinks. KONTY

British women, members of the Red Cross, provide coffee and donuts to the troops passing through. TAYNTON

British Valentine tanks at Ogbourne St. George, England. TAYNTON

The 70th receives new M4 medium tanks, Ogbourne St. George. TAYNTON

On 1 December 1943, by authority of Special Order No. 61 HQ Third Tank Group, the 70th was changed from a light tank battalion (three light tank companies) to a standard tank battalion (three medium tank companies, one light tank company, a headquarters company, and a service company). Companies A, B, and C were redesignated medium tank companies (M4 Sherman tanks), and a new company, Company D, was formed with light tanks (M5A1 Stuarts). The commanding officer for Company D was 1st Lt. Gordon R. Brodie, with 1st Lt. Walter T. Anderson as executive officer.

In February 1942, while still in the States, the original Company C had been detached and sent to Iceland as the 10th Light Tank Company. The 10th was then transferred to England about the same time as the arrival of the 70th and was deactivated, as indicated by the special orders shown below. Many of the 70th tankers enjoyed a reunion with their old buddies.

A 70th motor pool in England showing new M4 tanks to the left and half-tracks to the right. TAYNTON

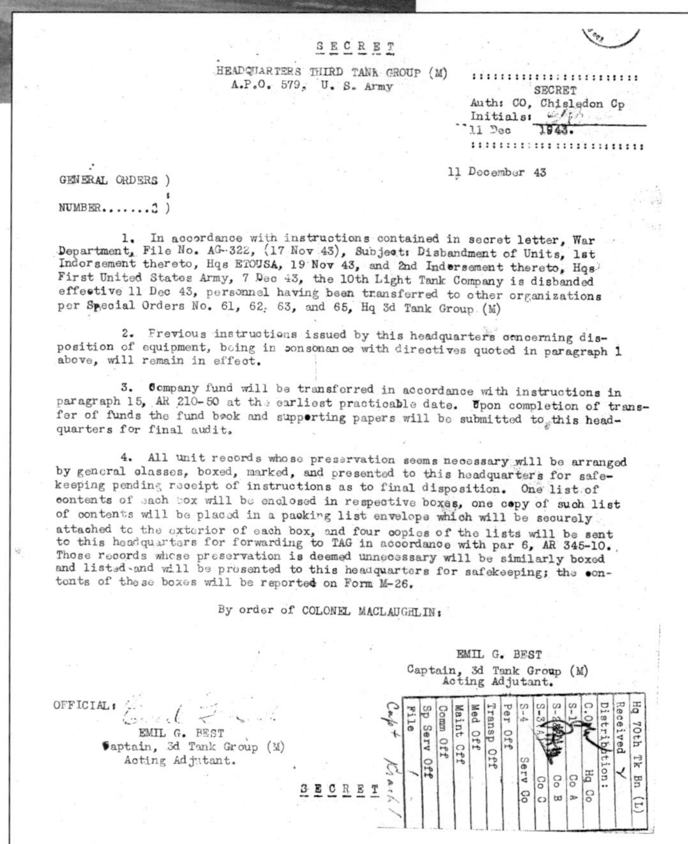

S E C R E T

HEADQUARTERS THIRD TANK GROUP (M)
A.P.O. 579, U. S. Army

SECRET
Auth: CO, Chisledon Cp
Initials:
11 Dec 1943.

GENERAL ORDERS)
NUMBER.......3)

11 December 43

1. In accordance with instructions contained in secret letter, War Department, File No. AG-322, (17 Nov 43), Subject: Disbandment of Units, 1st Indorsement thereto, Hqs ETOUSA, 19 Nov 43, and 2nd Indorsement thereto, Hqs First United States Army, 7 Dec 43, the 10th Light Tank Company is disbanded effective 11 Dec 43, personnel having been transferred to other organizations per Special Orders No. 61, 62, 63, and 65, Hq 3d Tank Group (M)

2. Previous instructions issued by this headquarters concerning disposition of equipment, being in consonance with directives quoted in paragraph 1 above, will remain in effect.

3. Company fund will be transferred in accordance with instructions in paragraph 15, AR 210-50 at the earliest practicable date. Upon completion of transfer of funds the fund book and supporting papers will be submitted to this headquarters for final audit.

4. All unit records whose preservation seems necessary will be arranged by general classes, boxed, marked, and presented to this headquarters for safekeeping pending receipt of instructions as to final disposition. One list of contents of each box will be enclosed in respective boxes, one copy of such list of contents will be placed in a packing list envelope which will be securely attached to the exterior of each box, and four copies of the lists will be sent to this headquarters for forwarding to TAG in accordance with par 6, AR 345-10. Those records whose preservation is deemed unnecessary will be similarly boxed and listed and will be presented to this headquarters for safekeeping; the contents of these boxes will be reported on Form M-26.

By order of COLONEL MACLAUGHLIN:

EMIL G. BEST
Captain, 3d Tank Group (M)
Acting Adjutant.

OFFICIAL:
EMIL G. BEST
Captain, 3d Tank Group (M)
Acting Adjutant.

S E C R E T

Hq 70th Tk Bn (L)
Received
Distribution:
C.O. Hq Co
S-1 Co A
S-2 Co B
S-3 Co C
S-4 Serv Co
Per Off
Transp Off
Med Off
Maint Off
Comm Off
Sp Serv Off
File

10th Light Tank Company (formerly Company C, 70th, from Iceland) deactivated. EISENHOWER PRESIDENTIAL LIBRARY

On 15 December 1943, eight medium tanks arrived and the tankers underwent extensive training to familiarize themselves with the new equipment. The M5A1 Stuart light tanks had automatic transmissions and were relatively easy to steer and drive. The new M4 Shermans (mediums) had standard transmissions, which required more skill to operate. The new tanks were also tougher to turn because of their weight (32 tons as opposed to 16 tons for a Stuart). On 23 December 1943, a waterproofing demonstration was held in Bideford, which initiated battalion preparations for amphibious operations.

On 16 February, the 70th moved to Camp Barton Stacey near Andover. Live-fire training was held at Castlemartin. Since the unit had obtained medium tanks, with .50-caliber and .30-caliber machine guns as standard equipment, live-fire training on both guns was required. Other weapons were also fired, including the 81mm mortar.

Live firing practice with .30- and .50-caliber guns, Castlemartin firing range, Pembroke, Wales. TAYNTON

British Valentine tank, England, 1944. NATIONAL ARCHIVES

Capt. Francis E. Songer, Lt. Orville K. Kirkpatrick, and Lt. Johnnie L. Casteel on their way to Torcross, England, April 1944. NATIONAL ARCHIVES

Live firing practice. TAYNTON

Mortar practice prior to D-Day, England, 1944. TAYNTON

DUPLEX DRIVE (DD) AMPHIBIOUS TANKS

On 4 March, Companies A and B started amphibious landing training using the new duplex drive (DD) tanks. Nicholas Straussler, a Hungarian engineer, came up with an idea to make a standard tank amphibious by designing a skirt to surround it and make it buoyant. An array of metal hoops and vertical rubber tubes were placed around the vehicle to act as a skeleton to support a canvas outer liner, very much like an Eskimo kayak. The water skirts were raised and lowered using air pressure in the vertical rubber tubes, which would straighten and stiffen to keep the skirt in place and become flexible when air pressure was decreased, thereby lowering the skirt. Two steerable inboard/outboard propulsion units were installed on the back of the tank to provide a forward speed of up to 4 knots. The tank would launch from a landing craft, travel to the shore, and be ready to support the landing force. The air pressure would be decreased and the skirt lowered to allow the main gun and machine guns to be brought to bear on targets. Then, at an opportune time, the vehicle would go to a "de-watering area" where the skirt and associated equipment were removed.

The canvas skirt worked adequately in moderate seas, but in wavy conditions it swamped easily. This was a big worry to 70th tankers: once water started pouring into the tank, it was very difficult to get out. The "Davis Lung," an underwater breathing apparatus, was supplied to units as a means of escape if the tank became submerged. Training using DD tanks was top secret, and no civilians were allowed to observe it.

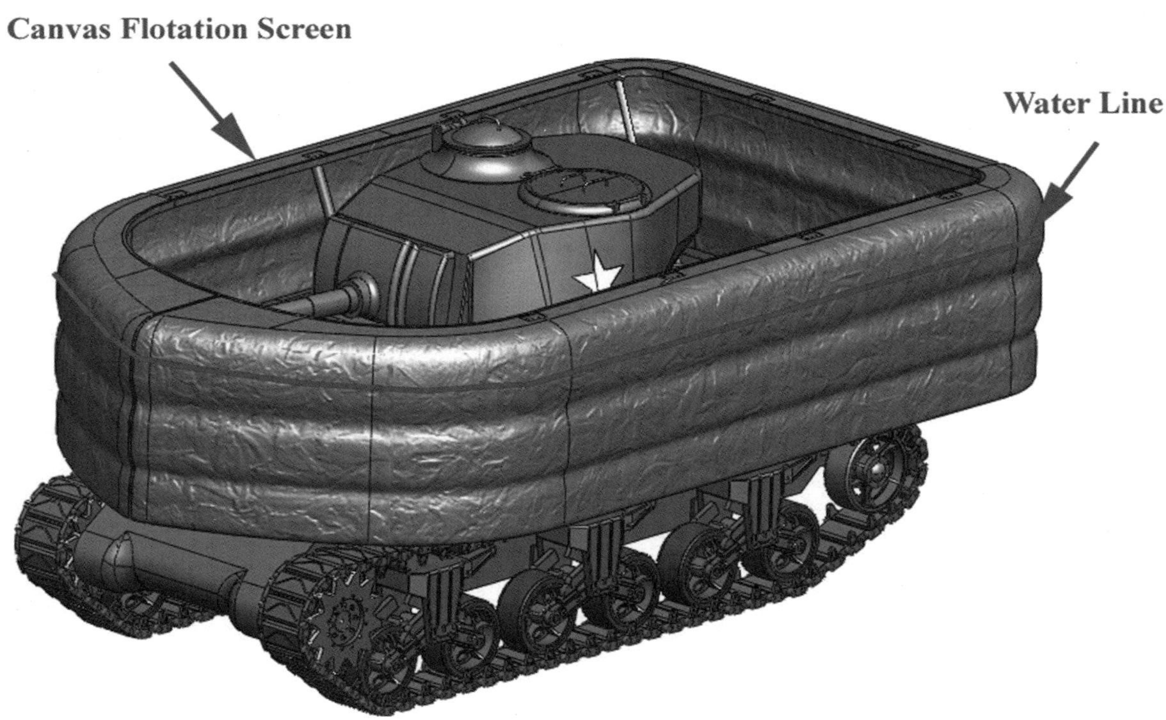

Drawing of the DD tank concept. A canvas shroud converted the tank into a watercraft, and two gearboxes with propellers were added to the rear of the tank. The purpose of the amphibious tank was to immediately provide support to infantry landing at Normandy without waiting for a Landing Ship, Tank (LST), to land. ROBERTS

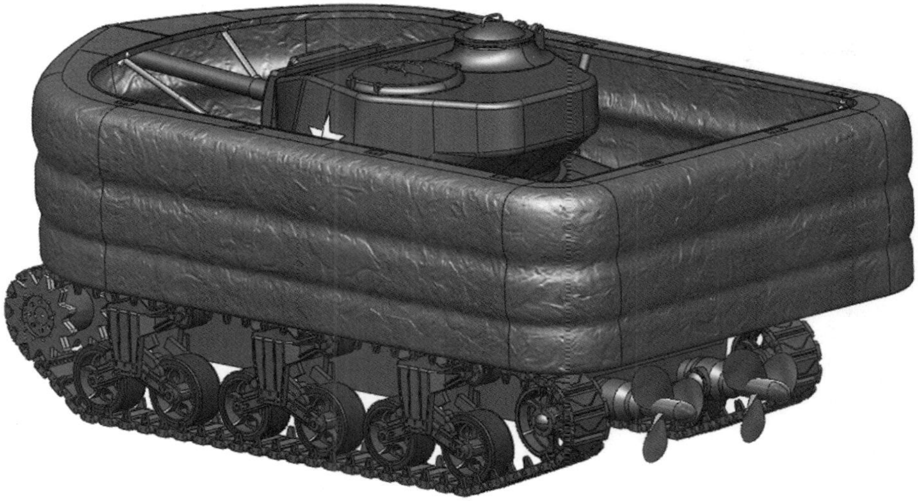

Drawing of a DD tank showing the propulsion units at the rear. ROBERTS

DD tanks practicing landing and embarkation at Slapton Sands, England, April 1944. The skirts are lowered. FRITZ

This rendering of a DD tank shows the inflatable skirt lowered. After landing, the tanks would move to a protected area for "de-watering" where the skirts were removed. It was often easy to identify a DD tank by the skirt framework that was usually still attached to the vehicle. Orders from command stated that no amphibious equipment was to be removed, but this proved impractical since the canvas skirt was a fire hazard during battle. ROBERTS

LCT 531 at Slapton Sands. FRITZ

LONDON

On 2 January 1944, Captain Taynton, along with other members of the 70th, visited London on a pass and took several photos of his travels. Wellington Barracks is the headquarters for the elite guards who protect British Royalty: the Grenadier, Coldstream, Scots, Irish, and Welsh guards. Typically the guards are dressed in tunics of gold-purled scarlet and tall bearskin caps, but during World War II they wore conventional military uniforms. Taynton also visited Eisenhower's headquarters at Grosvenor House, London. Barrage balloons above the headquarters were used to discourage enemy aircraft from low-level attacks.

British soldiers marching by Wellington Barracks, London, 1944. TAYNTON

Captain Taynton in front of Grosvenor House, Eisenhower's headquarters. Note the barrage balloon in the background. TAYNTON

Victoria Memorial in front of Buckingham Palace, London, 1944. TAYNTON

Lieutenant Colonel Welborn (left) and Capt. Robert McKericher (right). TAYNTON

Captain Taynton and Sergeant Vassey in front of the orderly room for Service Company, England, 1944. TAYNTO

Lt. Gordon Brodie (left) and Lt. Walter T. Anderson (right). BRODIE

Buckingham Palace, London, 1944. TAYNTON

Lt. Edward Jones (left) and Lieutenant Seeley (right). TAYNTON

London Metropolitan Policeman (Bobby), London, 1944. TAYNTON

Collegiate Church of St. Peter at Westminster Abbey (the Royals' private chapel), London, 1944. TAYNTON

London taxi at Ludgate Circus, 1944. The building in the background with the clock is Ludgate House. This is just down the road from St. Paul's Cathedral. The taxi is facing toward the River Thames. Capt. Ralph Lennon is on the left. TAYNTON

Regal Hotel in the background at the northeast corner of Hyde Park. This is a public forum for a variety of topics, typically political. The people standing on ladders are delivering speeches to whomever will listen. London, 1944. TAYNTON

Piccadilly Circus, 1944. TAYNTON

Yeoman Warder (Beefeater) of Her Majesty's Royal Palace and Fortress, the Tower of London. TAYNTON

Reindeer Officers Club, England, 1944. TAYNTON

Lieutenant Seeley in front of a fountain in the southeast corner of Hyde Park. TAYNTON

Tower of London. TAYNTON

TRAINING AND PREPARATION FOR THE INVASION

On 18 January 1944, the battalion was reviewed by Generals Montgomery, Lee, and Bradley. "Monty" gave a talk to the troops, which was informative and well received. Movement Order 36 commanded the 70th to relocate to Barton Stacey camps on 7 February 1944. The battalion was transferred to the 3rd Armored Group with the 741st and 743rd Battalions on 15 February. Companies A and B left for Pembrooke Range on 16 February.

On 21 March, the 70th was visited by Winston Churchill and General Eisenhower. Churchill was an energetic leader and traveled extensively to visit the various units in England with an inspiring message usually focused on defeating the "Hun."

From 20 to 22 March, a medium and light tank of the 70th participated in a test to gather information on bridge design at the 1106th Engineer Combat Group headquarters. Bridges were a problem in Europe in that they had a variety of capacities and conditions. The engineer combat groups were tasked with assessing the capacity of bridges and providing load rating signs to guide armored units to safely cross. The 1106th needed data on how to design bridges in anticipation of the landings in northern France. The 70th made several bridge crossings, helping the engineers develop design procedures for erecting bridges that could carry tanks.

During this period, various new ideas emerged on how to defeat the enemy bunkers that the troops expected to encounter on the beach at Normandy. At a demonstration for senior officers, the operators of a newly proposed rocket system were having difficulty penetrating a concrete wall. Lieutenant Colonel Welborn ordered three armor-piercing shells to be fired at the same point in the wall, which penetrated it satisfactorily, enough that the proposed rocket system was abandoned in favor of this technique. Maj. Gen. Percy Hobart, a British armored warfare expert, was given the task of developing specialized fighting vehicles for the impending invasion. General Hobart was instrumental in designing many new types of military equipment for the Normandy invasion, including the mine flail tank for clearing mines, the portable bridge for crossing obstacles, the flamethrower tank, and the duplex drive (DD) tank. The designs that were too radical and did not work were called the "funnies" by the troops. The U.S. Army adopted the DD amphibious tank.

Some 2.5-ton trucks of the 70th parked along a road in southern England. TAYNTON

On 18 April, the battalion received a D-Day list of vehicles and crew assignments. The troops spent 12–21 April practicing launching DD tanks from landing craft and simulated landing craft features. Leaks in the outer skirt fabric were identified and repaired. Many tanks with severe leaks had to be beached immediately to avoid being sunk. On 22 April, the battalion moved to Lupton Camp, on a high hill near the south coast of England, a short distance from Torquay on the English Channel. Tanks in Companies A and B were equipped with the canvas skirts and water propulsion units. Tanks with dozer blades were also provided to the 70th.

At that time, there were several tank units in the encampment, and the 70th tankers wanted to stand out since they had combat experience. They designed a mascot: a turtle named Joe Peckerwood, who wore a tanker's helmet and stood on top of the Earth, with a 75mm shell in one hand and saluting with the other. "Soixante-Dix" (French for "seventy") was on a banner across his chest, representing the 70th. Initially the turtle was standing on a swastika, but this was rejected in favor of the Earth. This mascot was painted on all 70th vehicles.

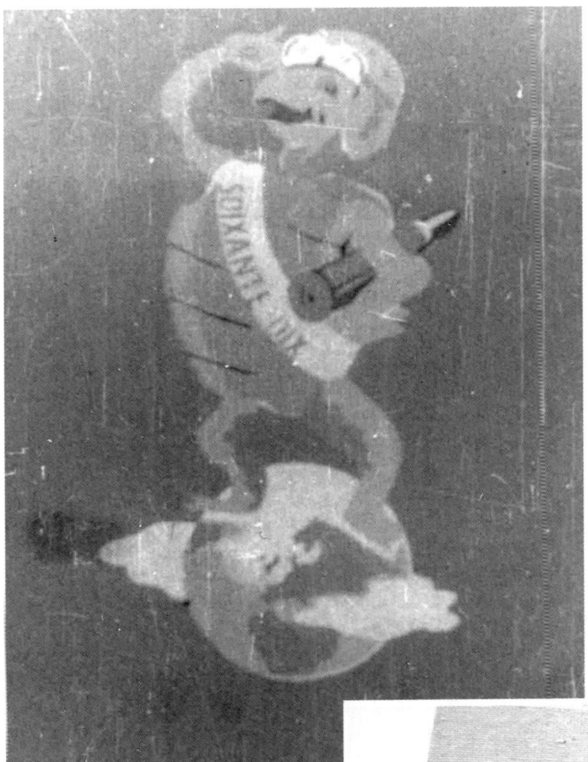

Joe Peckerwood. ERICKSON

Country home in England. Note the camouflaged military vehicles. Several of these homes were used to house Allied troops in preparation for D-Day. TAYNTON

Captain Taynton on a walkie-talkie (BC-611 radio) during maneuvers in England, 1944. TAYNTON

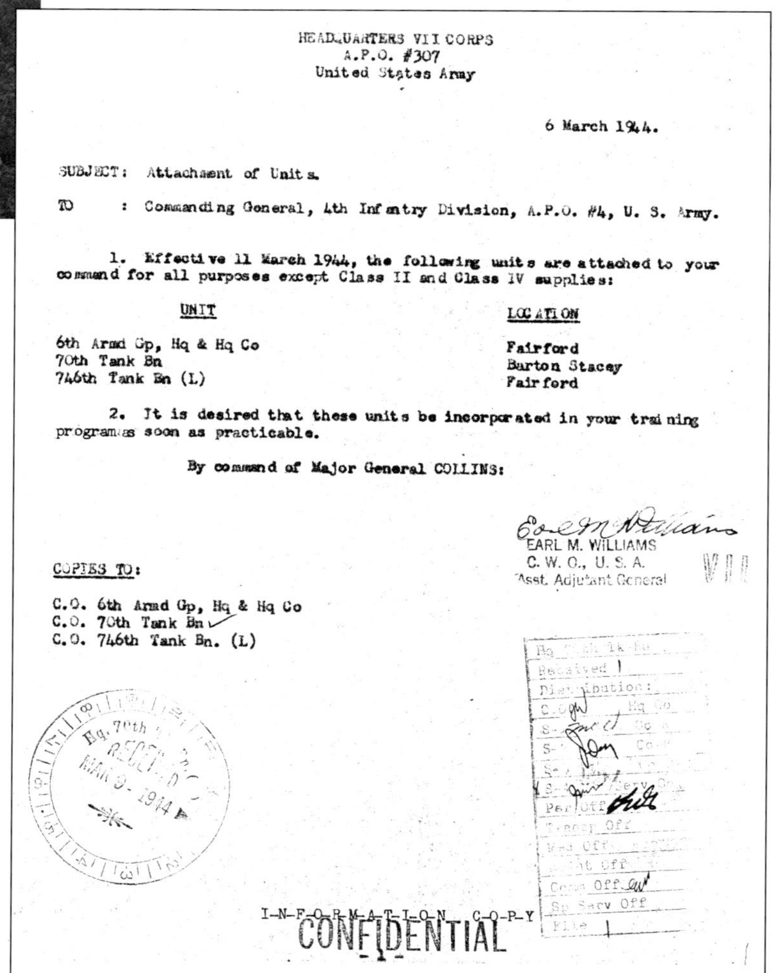

HEADQUARTERS VII CORPS
A.P.O. #307
United States Army

6 March 1944.

SUBJECT: Attachment of Units.

TO : Commanding General, 4th Infantry Division, A.P.O. #4, U. S. Army.

1. Effective 11 March 1944, the following units are attached to your command for all purposes except Class II and Class IV supplies:

UNIT	LOCATION
6th Armd Gp, Hq & Hq Co	Fairford
70th Tank Bn	Barton Stacey
746th Tank Bn (L)	Fairford

2. It is desired that these units be incorporated in your training program as soon as practicable.

By command of Major General COLLINS:

EARL M. WILLIAMS
C. W. O., U. S. A.
Asst. Adjutant General

COPIES TO:

C.O. 6th Armd Gp, Hq & Hq Co
C.O. 70th Tank Bn
C.O. 746th Tank Bn. (L)

I-N-F-O-R-M-A-T-I-O-N C-O-P-Y

CONFIDENTIAL

Order to attach the 70th to the 4th Division for D-Day. EISENHOWER PRESIDENTIAL LIBRARY

On 16 April, the 70th was moved to Camp Lupton, Devon. On 26 April, part of the 70th participated in a practice landing called Exercise Tiger at Slapton Sands in southwest England. The beaches were similar to those of Normandy. During the exercise, the Allied fleet was attacked by German E-boats (torpedo boats) out of Cherbourg, France. LSTs 507 and 531 were sunk. The exercise was considered a disaster, as 639 men were killed. Not only were experienced sailors and soldiers lost, but valuable ships with their materiel were also sunk. None of the 70th personnel or equipment was lost to enemy action; however, one Company A tank was sunk, two stopped running on the beach, and one stopped farther on shore. Upon recovering these vehicles, the 70th returned to Lupton Camp.

On 27 April, Generals Barton and Patton visited the 70th. On 6 May, General Roosevelt visited the bivouac area of the 70th. The general had proven to be a good friend to the 70th in Africa and Sicily. At this time, the 70th was ordered to be reorganized as a medium tank battalion with three companies of medium tanks (M4 Shermans) and one company of light tanks (M5A1 Stuarts). In mid-May, having conformed to the requirements for the standard U.S. Army tank battalion, the 70th was part of the large invasion force at the final staging areas nicknamed "sausage camps." On 13 May 1944, Colonel Wellborn was awarded the Legion of Merit for service in North Africa and Sicily.

Captain Taynton in front of his jeep in the English countryside, 1944. TAYNTON

M5 Light Tanks of Company D. BRODIE

ENGLAND

27 Nov/43	English Tank Camp	Ogbourne St. George, England
15 Feb/44	"D" Camp, Barton Stacey	Andover, England
22 Apr/44	Lupton Camp	Brixham, England
17 May/44	By Pass Camp	Exeter, England
18 May/44	Heathfield Camp, Honiton	Devonshire, England
27 May/44	Branksome Park Camp	Bournemouth, England
12 June/44	"C" Camp No. 6	Southhampton, England
14 June/44	LST 325	Port of Southhampton, England

70th camps in England. TAYNTON

On 17 May, Captain Taynton's detachment moved to Exeter (By Pass Camp), then on to Heathfield Camp near Honiton, Devonshire. The detachment was scheduled to arrive after D-Day. On 27 May, members of the detachment moved to private homes near the English Channel, 3 miles from Bournemouth. Large white stars were painted on the vehicles and turrets of the tanks, but these were later rubbed out with mud (in France), as they provided an easy reference point for German gunners.

The plan was to launch a 30-ton Sherman tank from a landing ship and drive it toward the shore like a watercraft. There was little freeboard (height above the waterline) with these canvas skirts, and vehicles were easily swamped and sunk. The driver of the tank sat in his normal seat while the rest of the crew sat on top of the tank to bail out in case it sank. Many 70th tankers were skeptical of the integrity of the water skirts and spent their own money to reinforce the fabric. On D-Day, most of the 70th tanks that were launched made it to shore because the seas were not as rough at Utah Beach as they were at Omaha Beach, where large waves swamped many of the DD tanks.

On the night of 4 June 1944, Companies A, B, C, and D were loaded on landing craft and moved offshore in preparation for the invasion. Headquarters Company and Service Company would follow later. Weather delayed the landing on the fifth, but a clearing developed and the order was given to proceed with the invasion on 6 June.

DD Tank #16 loaded onto an LCT backing away from shore, just prior to the invasion. The small extension ramps attached to the main LCT ramp were to ease the DD tanks into deep water to avoid swamping them. FRITZ

CHAPTER 5

Operation Overlord: The Invasion of Normandy

THE LANDING

The first three pages of the Utah Beach landing plan embody the overall plan for the 70th, with details down to company level. The code word "BIGOT" was the highest level of security, higher than top secret. Page 1, item 2, indicates that the 70th was attached to Regimental Combat Team 8 (CT8), which had as its core the 8th Infantry Regiment of the 4th Infantry Division. The landing plan on the following page shows that Company A was to land at a beach code-named "Tare Green," Company B at beach "Uncle Red," Company C at "Tare Green" and "Uncle Red," and Company D at "Uncle Red."

In front of Utah Beach, June 1944. TAYNTON

TOP SECRET - BIGOT NEPTUNE

SECRET
Auth: CG 4th Inf Div
Init: [initials]
Date: 27 May 1944.

HQ 70TH TANK BN
APO 579
27 May 1944.

Copy 11 of 11
Page 1 of 4

FO # 1

MAPS: France, CSGS 4250, Scale 1/50,000.
Sheets: 5E/2, 5E/4, 5E/6, 6E/1, 6E/3 & 4, 6E/5, 6E/6, 5F/2 6F/11.

France, CSGS 4347, Scale 1/25,000.
Sheets: 34-18NW, 34-18SW, 34-20SW, 31-21SE, 21-18NE, 31-18SE.

1. a. Enemy Situation - Intelligence Annex #2, FO #1, 4th Inf Div.

b. (1) The 4th Inf Division reinforced lands and assaults Utah Beach on D-day at H-hour and, in conjunction with the 90th Infantry Division, will seize CHERBOURG. (1020)

(2) CT8, reinforced, will land on beaches Tare (Green) and Uncle (Red), on a 2200 yard front, assault and breach the beach defenses thereon, and seize and secure the initial objective as shown on Annex #1.

2. The 70th Tank Bn, attached to the CT8, will land at H-hour on D-day on beaches Tare (Green) and Uncle (Red) and support the attack of the CT8.

3. a. Company "A" landing on Tare (Green) at H-hour (or as soon thereafter as practical) will assault the beach and provide continuous close support for the 1st Bn, CT8, within its zone of action. (See Annex #1)

b. Company "B" landing on the left of Company "A" on Uncle (Red) at H-hour (or as soon thereafter as practical) will assault the beach and provide continuous support for the 2nd Bn, CT8, within its zone of action. (See Annex #1)

c. Company "C" (less det. tankdozers) landing on Tare (Green) and Uncle(Red) at H plus 15, will support the attack of the 1st and 2nd Bn, CT8, within their respective zones of action. (See Annex #1)

d. Detachment, 4 tankdozers, Company "C" landing on Tare (Green) and Uncle (Red) at H plus 15 will assist the Beach Obstacle Task Force in accomplishing its mission (see Annex #9, FO #1, 4th Inf Div), thereafter revert to control of CT' on order.

TOP SECRET - BIGOT NEPTUNE

\- 1 -

REGRADED UNCLASSIFIED
ORDER SEC ARMY BY TAG/8807

TOP SECRET - BIGOT NEPTUNE
Page 2 of 4

e. Company "D" landing on Uncle (Red) at H plus 260 will proceed, as soon as possible, to its assembly area prepared to pass to the control of CG, 101st Airborne Division on order of CG, 4th Inf Div. (See Annex #1)

f. Remainder of Assault Elements will, after landing proceed immediately to rallying point (See Annex #1) unless assigned a mission provided for in par 3 x.

g. Reconnaissance Platoon on landing will initiate route and site reconnaissance to locate assault companies, battalion rallying point, maintenance point and rallying point of Company "D" (See Annex #1) and be prepared to lead these companies to their respective areas on call.

x. (1) The assault on TARE (Green) and UNCLE (Red) beaches will be pushed at all costs.

(2) The right five (5) tanks on beach TARE (Green) will initially provide flank protection for the 1st Bn, CT8.

(3) The left five (5) tanks on beach UNCLE (Red) will initially provide flank protection for the 2nd Bn, CT8.

(4) Company "C" will be prepared to fire at sea (approx 3000 yds) primarily to thefflanks of beach UTAH on order of Company Commander. Tanks will not fire over the heads of leading waves after H-5 minutes, but may fire on targets to the flanks if they can do so without endangering friendly troops. On landing the company will be prepared to fire to its respective flanks.

(5) Reconnaissance Platoon Leader will report on landing to the 4th Inf Div Beach Headquarters for information and instructions and be prepared to lead remaining elements of the command to their proper areas.

(6) All assault elements will make every effort to locate, contact and assist personnel of the 101st Airborne Division in their respective zones of action. Fire will be controlled to avoid firing on troops of the 101st Airborne Division.

(7) Contacts made with 101st Airborne Division and 82nd Airborne Division will be reported by time and place to CP of supported infantry commanders without delay.

(8) Vehicles returning from the front will evacuate wounded.

(9) Watches will be synchronized prior to embarkation and checked with accurate ship time, if available, prior to landing.

(10) Only those parts of this order applicable to a company or detachment will be carried ashore by that company or detachment.

4. Administrative Plan. (See Annex #4, FO #1, 4th Infantry Division.)

TOP SECRET - BIGOT NEPTUNE

\- 2 -

TOP SECRET - BIGOT NEPTUNE
Page 3 of 4

5. Signal Communication (See Annex #5, FO #1, 4th Infantry Division).

a. Initial C.P. ashore.

(1) Vicinity of HOUDIENVILLE (4394).

(2) Company C P's to be reported.

b. Radio Communication.

(1) Radio silence will be maintained until H-hour unless upon order of CG, VII Corps.

(2) Company commanders of Companies "A" and "B" will maintain a listening watch on VII Corps net from H minus 2 hours to time of launching at which time will revert to normal communication channels.

(3) Company "D" will use normal communication channels until attached to 101st Airborne Division, at which time Company Commander will switch to Airborne communication channel.

(4) Communication will be maintained with 6th Armored Group upon attachment.

c. Visual Signals.

(1)

Smoke	Pyrotechnic	Meaning
Orange of Yellow	Single Yellow Star (AN-44)	"Cease Fire on This Area"
Red		"Start or Resume Supporting Tank or Heavy Weapons Fire Against This Point"
Violet		"Clear Area for Demolition Charge"

(2) Panels: Any ORANGE display by panel (AP-50-A), flag or cloth means "I Am Friendly".

(3) Lights: Three (3) dots or three (3) dashes using signal lamp or flashlight means "I Am Friendly".

JOHN C. WELBORN,
Lt. Col., 70th Tank Bn,
Commanding.

Annex #1 - Operations Overlay

TOP SECRET - BIGOT NEPTUNE

\- 3 -

Utah Beach landing plan.

NATIONAL ARCHIVES

The maps to be used by the 70th were the Geographical Section General Staff (GSGS) (MI4) maps from the Directorate of Military Survey, War Office, London 1943, #4250, scale 1/50,000. These maps, developed by the British, were a standard at the Normandy invasion. They were divided into several sheets and used with onion-skin paper overlays to describe tactical situations in the field.

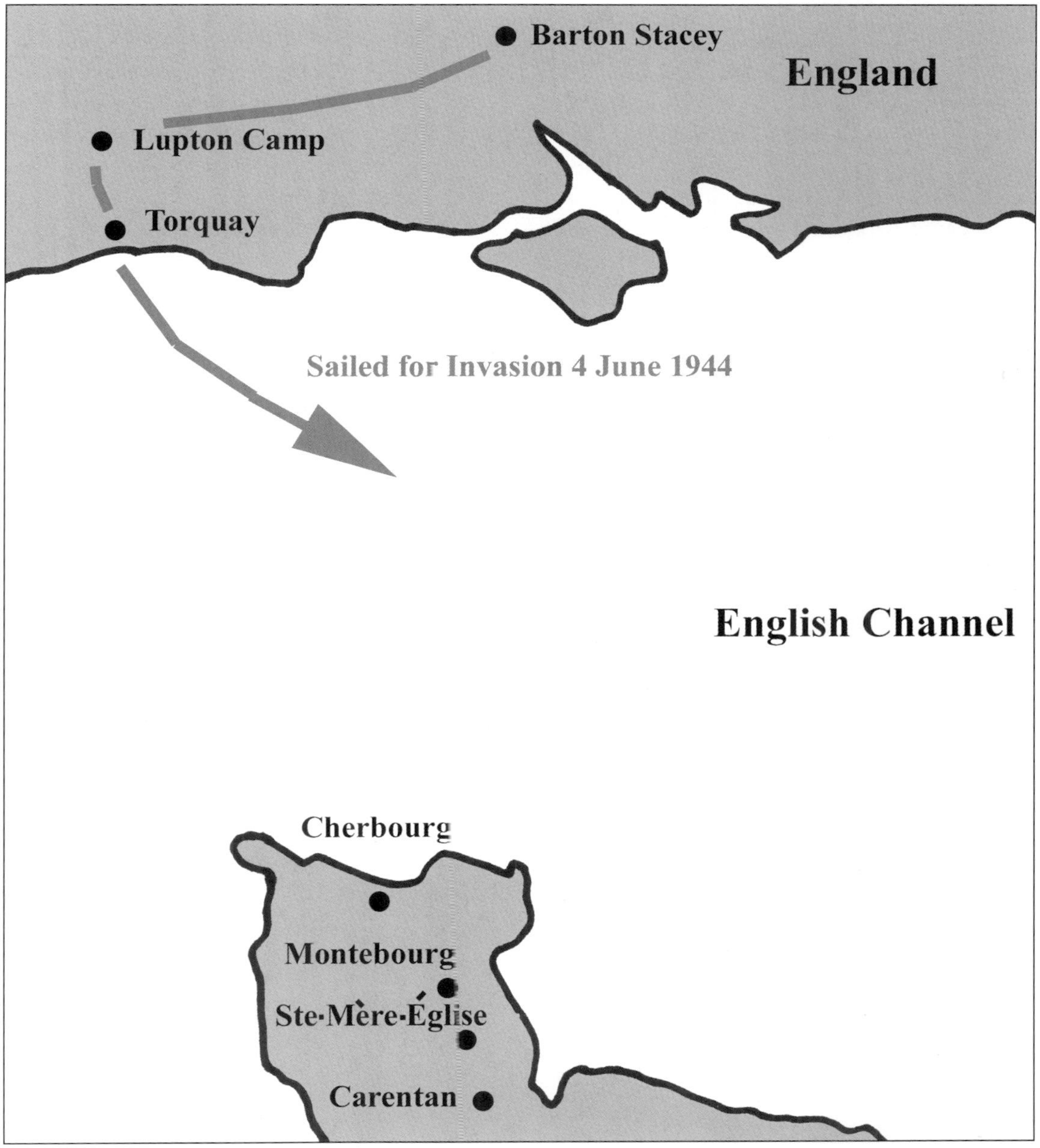

Map showing embarkation from England. ROBERTS

Unfavorable weather plagued the initiation of the Overlord operation, arguably the most complex amphibious landing in the history of warfare at that time. Since ocean tidal actions were favorable for a landing and such a condition would not exist again for several weeks, the order was given to load landing craft and prepare for the invasion. On 3 June 1944, the 70th Tank Battalion was ordered to ports of embarkation in Devonshire County, England.

Company A loaded LCTs 592, 593, 594, and 595. Company B loaded LCTs 510, 531, 596, and 597. LCT 510 was loaded with tanks B6 through B9 and 2nd Platoon, Company B leader Lieutenant Casteel and crews. LCT 531 was loaded with tanks B1 through B4 with Lieutenant Kirkpatrick and the 1st Platoon, Company B. LCT 596 was loaded with tanks B5, B10, B15, and B16 with Captain Songer and crews from various platoons. LCT 597 was loaded with tanks B11 through B14 with Lieutenant Townsend, 3rd Platoon leader, Company B, and crews.

Company D loaded onto three LCTs. LCT 2424 contained the 1st Platoon, Company D, plus tanks D15, D16, and the T-2 recovery vehicle. LCT 2040 was loaded with the 2nd and 3rd Platoons of Company D, minus Tank D15. LCT 2135 was loaded with vehicles of the 4th Reconnaissance Troop along with Tank D17. Companies A, C, and D departed from Dartmouth. Company B departed from Torcross.

After loading the LCTs, the 70th sailed out of the harbor at approximately 1645 on 3 June and joined the invasion convoy. The 70th was assigned to land on Utah Beach, on the Cotentin Peninsula. The other major landing beaches were Omaha (American), Juno (Canadian), Gold (British), and Sword (British), all east of the 70th's landing beach. Because of the weather delay and stormy conditions in the English Channel, many of the tankers became seasick and began to care little about where they were heading. They spent 4 and 5 June in a holding pattern off Portsmouth, England, in rough seas. According to the

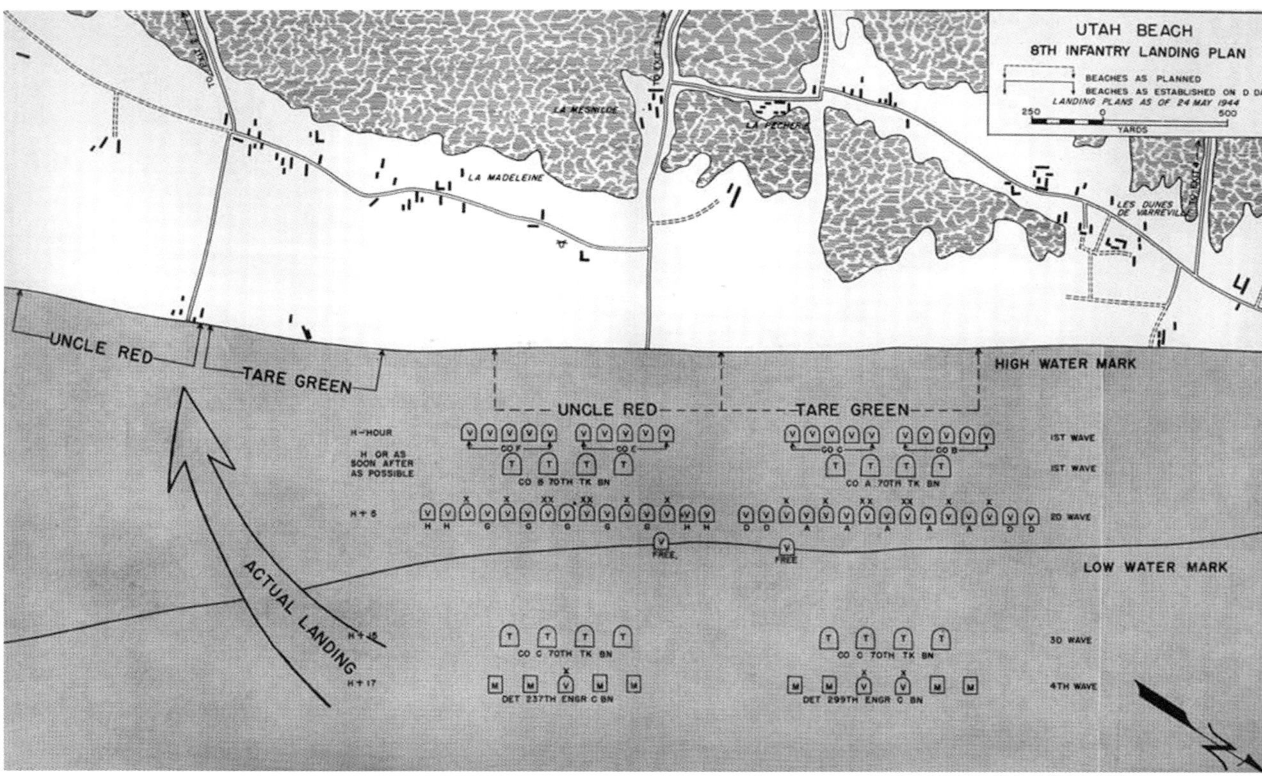

In the landing plan at Utah Beach, showing both the planned and the actual landing zones, the arrow points to one of the beach exits, Exit 2, which was the primary avenue of egress from Utah Beach used by the 70th. Company D (not shown on the landing plan) landed last and traveled inland to support the 101st Airborne Division southwest of Vierville. 70TH HISTORY

Company B diary, by this time most of the 70th crewmembers were seasick and not up to having a meal with the 10-in-1 rations on board ship. At about 0300 on 6 June, during a lull in the weather, bombardment of the French coast began and everyone watched the "show." C47 transport aircraft were seen retiring from the Normandy area.

At 0500, word was given to prepare for landing. The tank engines were started and warmed up while the water skirts on the DD tanks were made ready for launching. Tank engines used in World War II required warming up in order to operate smoothly when needed. A cold engine could sputter, foul up the spark plugs, and stall at a critical time. Many crews went to the galley to get a cup of hot coffee before launching the DDs. After an air corps bombing attack on the beach, accompanied by heavy gunfire from Allied battleships, the 70th launched the DD tanks in rough seas in support of Combat Team 8.

USS *Nevada* (BB-36), 27,550 tons displacement, 583 feet in length, and carrying ten 14-inch guns and twenty-one 5-inch guns. It was a survivor of the Pearl Harbor attack and was refloated and refitted to provide artillery support for D-Day. Here the *Nevada* rides at anchor on or about 15 June 1944. TAYNTON

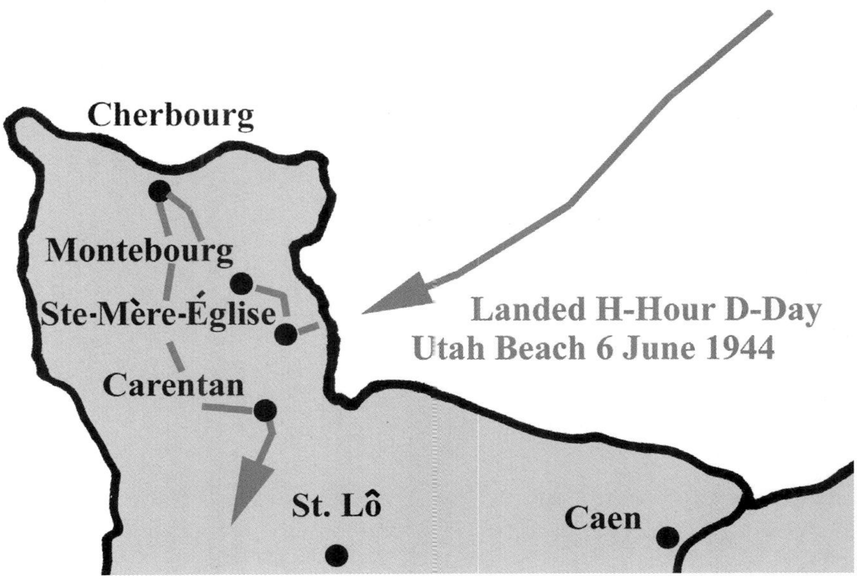

Approximate route of the 70th through Normandy and on to Paris, 1944. ROBERTS

View of Utah Beach, approximately D+1,when Headquarters Company landed. ERICKSON

The sole 70th Tank Battalion survivor of the sinking of LCT 592, 1st Sgt. Glen Gibson, is shown at the end of the war in front of a 2.5-ton truck in Nuremberg, Germany, 1945. ERICKSON

LCT 2135 on the way to Utah Beach showing Tank #17 of Company D, 70th Tank Battalion (mid-photo on left). Tank #17 was commanded by the executive officer, Walter T. Anderson. The navy identification number for this LCT was 2135, while the army designation number was 278. The personnel are listening to the address from General Eisenhower regarding the invasion. The remaining vehicles are of the 4th Reconnaissance Troop, 4th Infantry Division. PETER CROSS COLLECTION

LCT 2135 starting to unload at Utah Beach, apparently in deep water since the vehicle at the bow is nearly submerged.
PETER CROSS COLLECTION

The guideboat for the LCTs carrying Company A was hit and sank immediately. A signal was given to form up on LCT 593 prior to launching the DDs. On the way in, LCT 592 (carrying four tanks of 2nd platoon, Company A) struck a mine, broke in two, and sank. Only one out of twenty 70th tankers (Sergeant Gibson) survived the sinking of LCT 592. Tank A6 was hurled about a hundred feet into the air as a result of the explosion. LCTs 593, 594, and 595 started launching DDs at about 0600, approximately four thousand yards from the beach. Tank A16, first to be launched, sank at about 0614 as a result of sea motion from a craft firing rockets nearby. All other tanks reached shore, with Tank A3 being the first at 0632. Sgt. Henry V. Nothel of Tank A3 was first to fire on an enemy position after breeching the seawall. Tanks A3, A5, and A11 were stuck in mud along with dozer Tank DT1. It is not clear when and where they got stuck. Company A then formed up with 1st Battalion, 8th Infantry Regiment, 4th Infantry Division, and moved to Ste.-Marie-du-Mont to dewaterproof and reorganize. Company B landed successfully and advanced toward Ste.-Marie-du-Mont. Company B tanks B2 and B16 were disabled on the causeway near the beach. Company C landed with dozer tanks and conventional tanks with water fording gear, which was different from the DD tanks. The fording gear allowed the vehicle to travel in deep water with intake and engine exhaust vents, but not to float like a DD tank. Company C was supposed to land after Companies A and B, but due to the "fog of war" it landed first. The force proceeded through Les Dunes de Varreville on the road to St. Martin-de-Varreville.

An M4 Sherman named *Cannon Ball*. This is Tank #2 from Company C of the 70th Tank Battalion. It appears to have been swamped in a depression (probably a projectile impact crater). This vehicle was recovered, repaired, and in use in northern France. Note the Joe Peckerwood mascot on the left front side. U.S. ARMY

Troop attack transport (APA) and cargo attack transport (AKA) ships viewed from Utah Beach in the vicinity of Exit 2. ERICKSON

Dozer tank *Double Trouble* from the 70th Tank Battalion at Utah Beach. U.S. ARMY

Upon landing, tanks from Companies A, B, and C moved inland, clearing out pillboxes and enemy pockets of resistance. There was a huge traffic jam at Exit 2 since the Germans had flooded the countryside, and the roads were the only way inland toward initial objectives. Many of the infantry soldiers had to wade through water to get farther inland. The battalion overcame obstacles such as blown bridges, and moved up in support of the 8th Infantry Regiment. At the end of the day, Company A reached the objective at Turqueville and Companies B and C reached their objectives near Pouppeville. On the first day of operations, the 70th lost sixteen medium tanks, eight of them at sea. Casualties (both KIA and MIA) of the sinking of the LCT were 2nd Lt. William S. Kline and the following enlisted men: Sgt. John A. Callahan, Sgt. John W. Clarke, T/4 Glenn E. Bergstreser, T/4 Bert J. Clear, Cpl. Albert J. Jensen, Cpl. Stanley J. Marszalek, Cpl. Donald R. Neal, Cpl. Nicholas W. Rhimer, T/5 Francis W. Goble, T/5 Guadalupe P. Hernandez, PFC Lawrence J. Coughlin, PFC Hugh S. Gosnell, Pvt. Norman B. Foster, Pvt. Stephen W. Jaskulski, Pvt. Charles E. Metz, Pvt. Robert H. Moyer, Pvt. Gerard K. O'Brien, and Pvt. Lewis Saray.

Others were lost along the causeways toward the objective to antitank fire and mines. Company D immediately moved inland to support the 101st Airborne Division, which landed at drop zones near Saint-Côme-du-Mont. Contact with friendly forces in the 101st zone was difficult because the Airborne Division was scattered, causing difficulty in communicating with the 101st headquarters.

Company A DD tank disabled on one of the causeways from Utah Beach. U.S. ARMY

DD Tank just inland from Utah Beach carrying soldiers. U.S. ARMY

U.S. Waco glider located in a field in Normandy. ERICKSON

LST arriving at Utah Beach and its ramp being lowered. A navy officer (farthest away in the photo) is directing the unloading of the ship. ERICKSON

On the way to Utah Beach, with an LST on the left and a badly damaged troop transport (APA) on the right. ERICKSON

LCT 533 unloads in deep water. A 2.5-ton truck and another vehicle were swamped as a result of a rapidly rising tide or engine problems. ERICKSON

This 2.5-ton truck and ammunition trailer either got stuck or the engine quit just as the tide was coming in. The tidal levels at Utah Beach varied significantly, often trapping vehicles. ERICKSON

Despite snorkel equipment, this jeep was caught in the rising tide during landing, or possibly the engine quit. ERICKSON

Approaching what appears to be Exit 2. The date is 15 June 1944. The beachhead had been established with barrage balloons along the coast. TAYNTON

Utah Beach, 15 June, during Captain Taynton's detachment's arrival at Normandy. LST 523 struck a mine on 19 June and sank. It was carrying twenty Sherman tanks and is now a popular diving site. LST 230 participated in the Normandy landings and then sailed to the coast of southern France, where it participated in Operation Dragoon. TAYNTON

DEAD MAN'S CORNER

On 6 June 1944, while Companies A, B, and C were attacking to the north and west of Exit 2, Company D supported the 101st Airborne in the vicinity of Vierville, which is southwest of Exit 2. Company D, equipped with the light tank M5A1, aided the 101st by knocking out pockets of enemy resistance such as machine-gun positions and roadblocks. There were no defined enemy lines and the tactical situation was fluid. Company D tanks were subjected to attacks by handheld antitank weapons.

This M5A1 light tank from Company D, 70th Tank Battalion, is Tank #12, as indicated on the armor in front of the controlled differential unit. It was disabled by German antitank fire on 7 June 1944 at the junction of Highway D913 and N13, resulting in the death of one or more crewmembers. Several 101st soldiers indicated that while engaged in fighting the enemy on 7 June, they saw a deceased crewman in the tank. Due to fighting in the area where opposing lines were not well defined, tank crewmembers killed in action were not recovered for several days. This junction became known as Dead Man's Corner. This photo has been published in several books on World War II. U.S. ARMY

For many years, historical discussions have centered around the identity of the dead man in Tank D12. The following analysis sheds light on who may have been in the tank on 7 June.

Capt. Gordon R. Brodie was the commander of Company D during Operation Overlord. Company D landed at Utah Beach on 6 June and was assigned to the 101st Airborne Division, which was engaged with German infantry in and around Saint-Côme-du-Mont as well as other small towns in the area. Captain Brodie most likely delegated the writing of the Company D diary to a company clerk who made entries, but not necessarily on the date the event occurred. Battalion headquarters had mandated that unit activities be documented for future historical records.

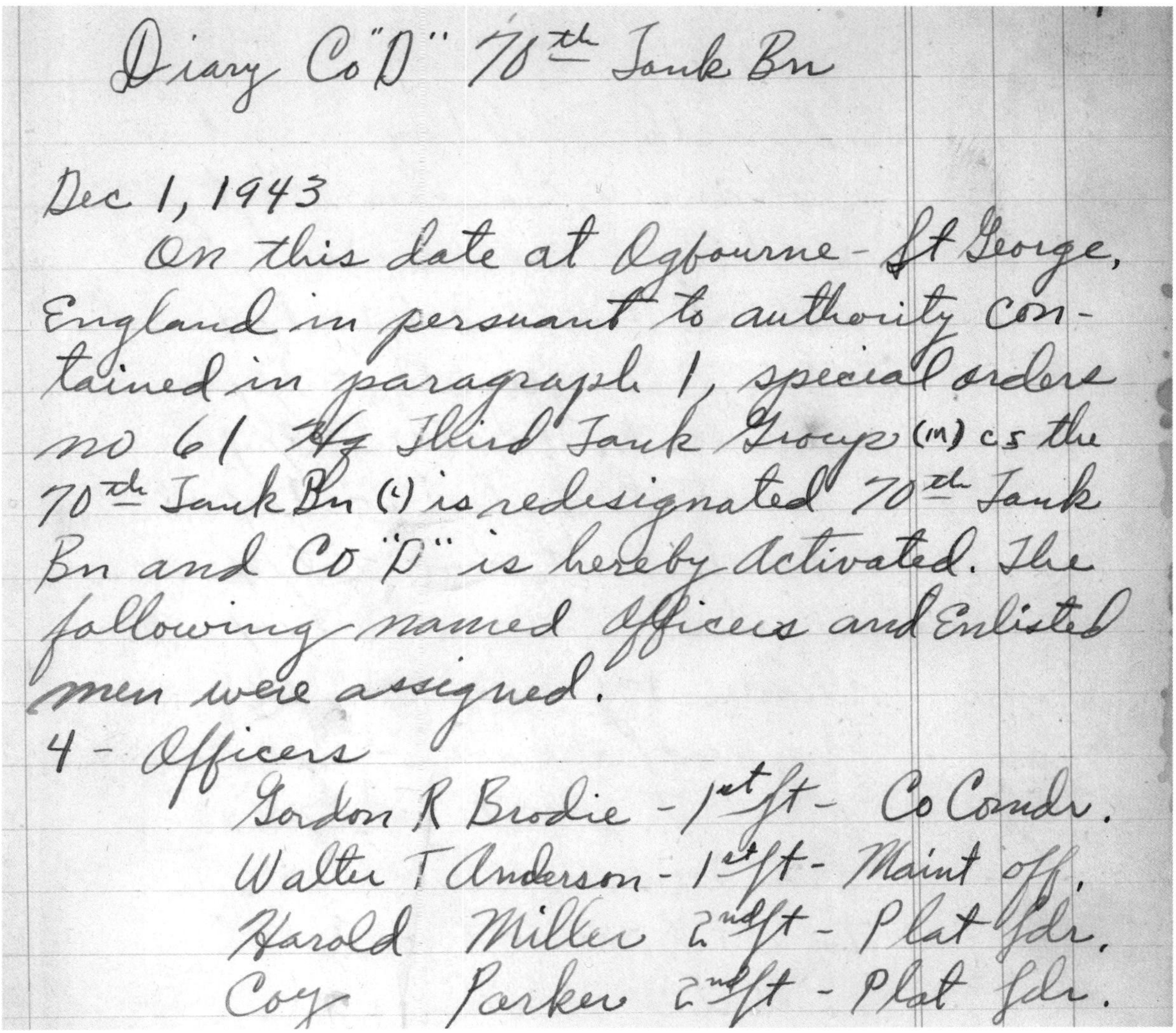

Diary Co "D" 70th Tank Bn

Dec 1, 1943
On this date at Ogbourne-St George, England in persuant to authority contained in paragraph 1, special orders no 61 Hq Third Tank Group (M) cs the 70th Tank Bn (L) is redesignated 70th Tank Bn and Co "D" is hereby activated. The following named Officers and Enlisted men were assigned.

4 - Officers
Gordon R Brodie - 1st Lt - Co Comdr.
Walter T Anderson - 1st Lt - Maint off.
Harold Miller 2nd Lt - Plat Ldr.
Coy Parker 2nd Lt - Plat Ldr.

A Company D diary entry notes that the company was reconstituted on 1 December 1943 and that 1st Lt. Walter T. Anderson was assigned to the unit as the maintenance officer. Since he was a first lieutenant but not the company commander, he was the executive officer, the second highest rank in the company. TAYNTON

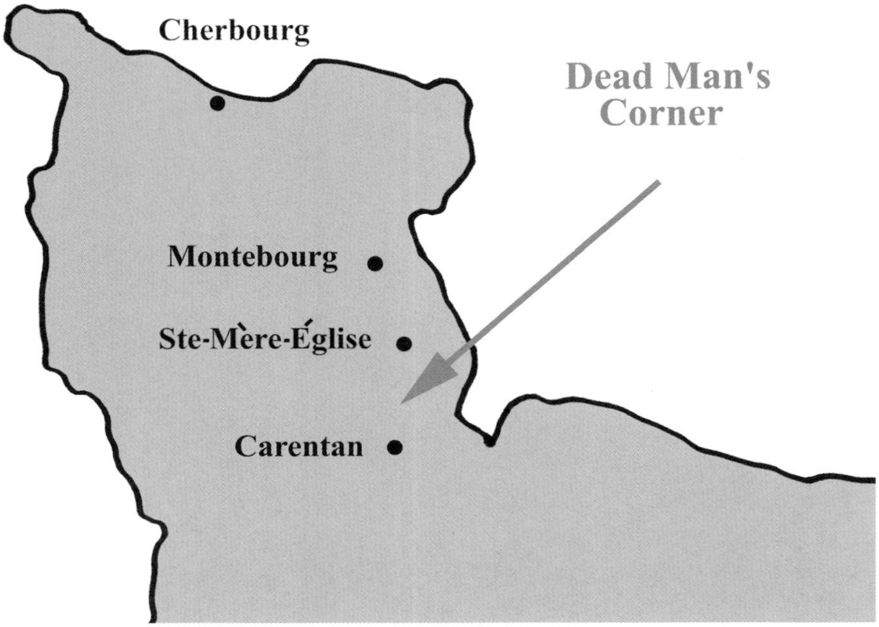

Location of Dead Man's Corner, just north of Carentan and southwest of Vierville. ROBERTS

Captain Brodie. TAYNTON

An S-4 report (logistics material report) showed two D Company tanks lost as of D+2 (June 8). One of these is Tank #12. D Company clerk documentation lists an entry on 14 June that Sgt. Anthony Tomasheski and Pvt. Aaron D. Curry were killed in action on 7 June. The morning reports were written in England at the time, since many of the support units had not yet arrived. The 14 June report shows Sergeant Tomasheski and Private Curry killed in action on 7 June. The morning report lists 1st Lt. Walter T. Anderson killed in action on 8 June. Individual Deceased Personnel Files (IDPF) show 1st Lieutenant Anderson's date of death to be 8 June, Sergeant Tomasheski's 7 June, and Private Curry's 7 June.

From 6 June to 8 June, D Company was attached to the 101st and immediately traveled toward Vierville. On 7 June, two light tanks were lost during engagements supporting the 101st southwest of Vierville. Tank #12 was destroyed by antitank fire, while Tank #10 appeared to have been hit by a large-caliber projectile but was later repaired. Sgt. Frank E. McNally, Sergeant Tomasheski, and Private Curry were killed.

From the history of the 70th Tank Battalion, the fact that only two light tanks were destroyed on the second day is consistent with Tanks #10 and #12 referenced in the Company D diary. Tanks #10 and #12 were disabled on 7 June. Tankers with date of death on that date are likely crewmembers of Tank #10 or #12. Three tankers (Private Curry—KIA, Pvt. Jack Hughes—WIA, and Sergeant Tomasheski—MIA) are mentioned as being a mile northeast of Carentan, which is consistent with the approximate location of Tank #12, although Dead Man's Corner is located north of Carentan, rather than northeast. There are no roads northeast of Carentan where the 70th traveled. Private Curry is probably one of the crewmembers of Tank #12, since he had received tank training and a tank driver badge while in England. He died from severe burns on 7 June, which is consistent with an antitank rocket attack as shown in the U.S. Army photo of Tank #12 on page 134. Private Hughes is a possible survivor of Tank #12 (assistant driver). Sergeant Tomasheski is reported MIA at the same location as Private Curry. According to the casualty lists in the *History of the 70th Tank Battalion*, morning reports, and the IDPF, Sergeant Tomasheski was killed on 7 June 1944 and is probably the commander of Tank #12.

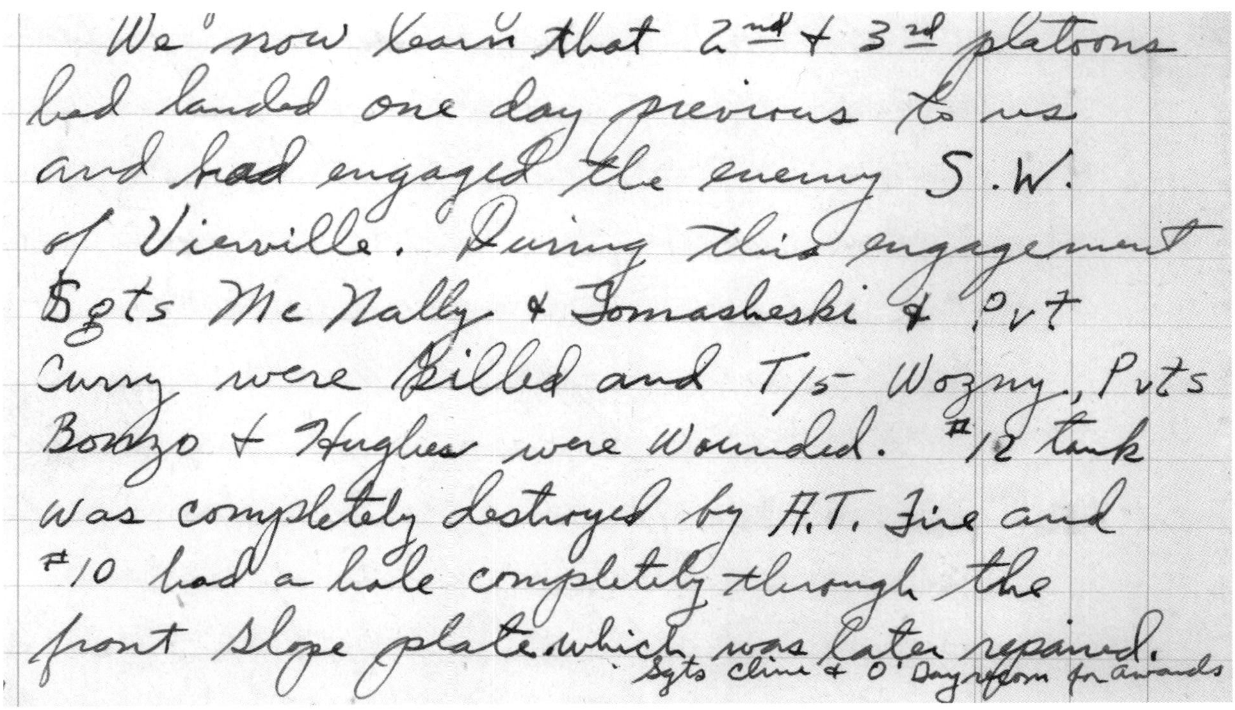
We now learn that 2nd + 3rd platoons had landed one day previous to us and had engaged the enemy S.W. of Vierville. During this engagement Sgts McNally + Tomasheski + Pvt Curry were killed and T/5 Wozny, Pvts Bozzo + Hughes were wounded. #12 tank was completely destroyed by A.T. fire and #10 had a hole completely through the front slope plate which was later repaired.
Sgts Cline + O'Day up for awards

Company D diary entry dated 8 June 1944. TAYNTON

T/4 Francis Ross (third from left), driver of T2 tank retriever *Dangling Destiny*, in France with civilians, 1944. The T2 was converted from an old Lee tank. The 75mm main gun is a fake. ROSS

There were two tiers of enlisted ranks in the U.S. Army during World War II. There was technician grade, which would be a specialist (engine mechanic, tank driver, ammunition technician, etc.), and command grade. Ranks of a regular sergeant or corporal were command grades who had authority to command troops. T grades such as T/3, T/4, and T/5 were technicians and did not have command authority in a tank company. Typically, a T-grade enlisted man was with maintenance or some specialty that supported the company. T/4 Ross was the driver of a T2 tank retriever since he was considered a skilled driver. The T2 retriever was a specialty maintenance vehicle that reported to Headquarters Company only. A typical light-tank crew consisted of a driver (technician grade), assistant driver (private), gunner (corporal), and commander/loader (sergeant). Privates were occasionally used as drivers for tanks. It should be noted that some gunners were corporals, which differed from the then-current U.S. Army Table of Organization & Equipment.

According to the Company D diary, those killed in action from 2nd and 3rd Platoons were Sgt. Frank E. McNally, Sgt. Anthony I. Tomasheski, and Pvt. Aaron D. Curry. Tank #12 was in 3rd Platoon. Tank #17 had been missing but was later found along with the body of 1st Lieutenant Anderson. The mention of the knocked-out Tank #17 and death of 1st Lieutenant Anderson in the same sentence in the Company D diary suggests that the events are related.

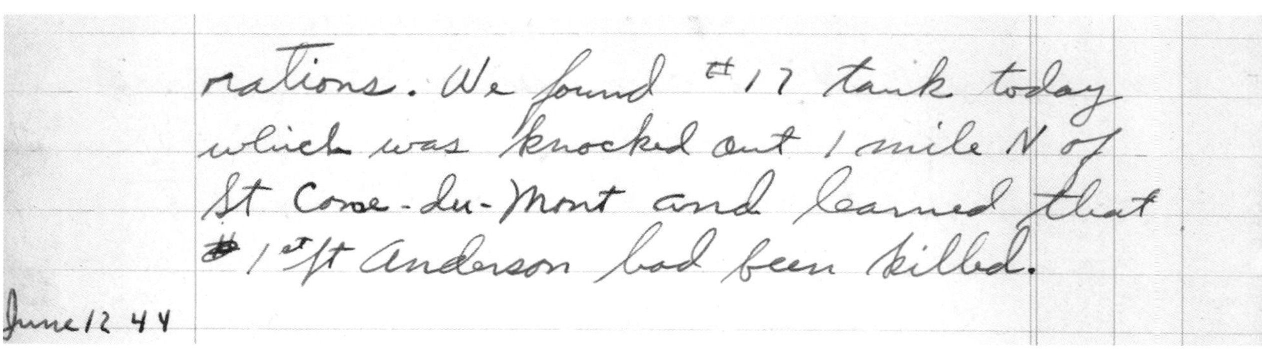

rations. We found #17 tank today
which was knocked out 1 mile N of
St Come-du-Mont and learned that
1st Lt Anderson had been killed.
June 12 44

Company D diary entry 11 June: 1st Lieutenant Anderson killed in action. TAYNTON

Since platoons of the 70th were often split up between infantry units, it was not unusual for a company commander not to immediately know of information on 70th casualties. Also, enemy lines were undefined in this area, making communications difficult. Since Tank #17 was the only 70th tank on LCT 2135, it most likely got separated from D Company upon landing.

T/5 Ross was in the headquarters section and knew 1st Lieutenant Anderson. An excerpt from the biography of Francis Ross recounts that Anderson was a tank commander and wanted Ross to be his driver. Ross preferred to stay with the T2 tank retriever. In a telephone interview conducted by the author with Francis Ross, he stated that Anderson was in Tank #17. Since Anderson was the executive officer, it would be logical that he would be in Tank #17, as it was in the headquarters section. The Ross diary also indicates that 1st Lieutenant Anderson was killed by a mortar round landing directly on the turret of his tank. Tank #12 was disabled by antitank rocket fire.

The weapon penetration near the driver's compartment in the U.S. Army photo (see page 134) is consistent with that of an antitank rocket attack. The simulated photo of the likely orientation of the Panzerfaust projectile location (see photo below) shows a probable impact point on Tank #12. Note that this penetration is right by the driver's head, and a shaped charge would most likely have killed the driver. It should also be noted that the tank hatch on the driver's side in the U.S. Army photo is not open and is probably locked, since an unlocked hatch tends to bounce, increases the difficulty in viewing through the hatch periscope, and interferes with turret traverse. This suggests that the deceased driver was probably still in the driver's seat when this photo was taken. The right-side assistant driver's hatch is open, suggesting that the assistant driver escaped.

Other crewmembers may have also sustained wounds from the antitank attack. Although Sergeant McNally was killed on 7 June in the vicinity of Dead Man's Corner, the description of how he died (sniper fire) does not appear to be consistent with riding in a tank that was suddenly hit by an antitank rocket.

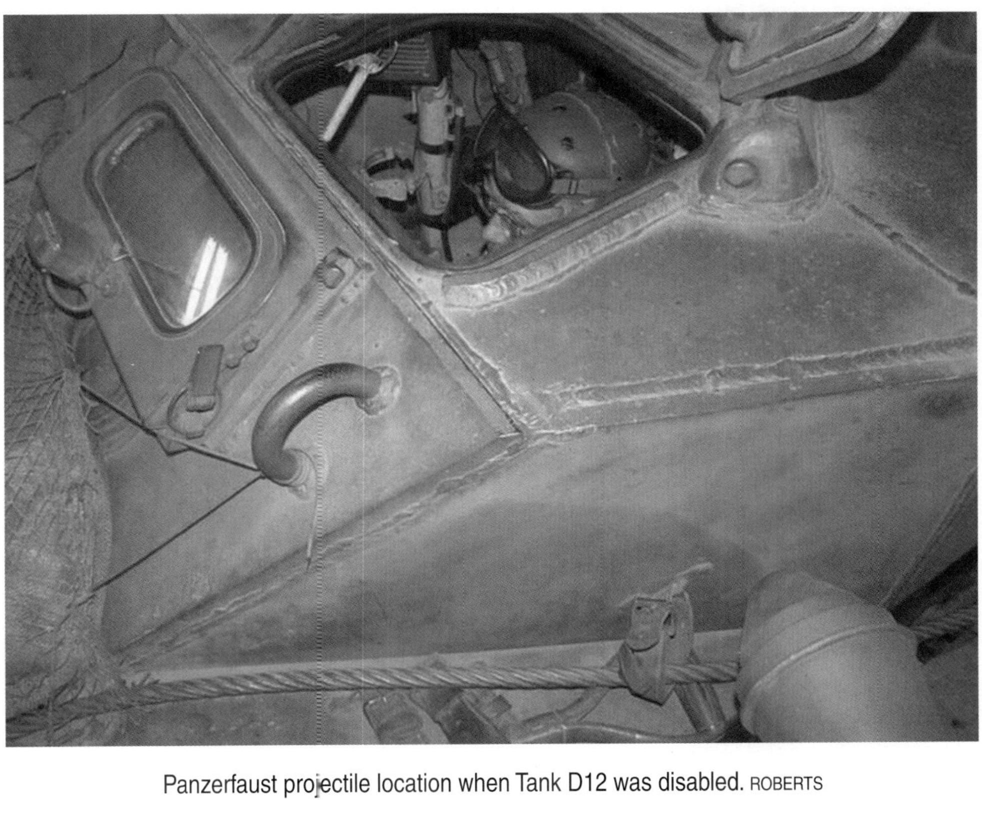

Panzerfaust projectile location when Tank D12 was disabled. ROBERTS

The preponderance of the evidence indicates that 1st Lieutenant Anderson—who was listed in the IDPF, morning report, and *History of the 70th Tank Battalion* as killed by mortar fire on 8 June—was actually killed while commanding Tank #17, not as a crewmember of Tank #12. Private Curry and Sergeant Tomasheski are most likely crewmembers of Tank #12. Tomasheski is the likely commander of Tank #12. Curry was most likely still in the tank and may be the dead man from which Dead Man's Corner got its name. Tomasheski may have escaped since the commander's hatch is open and the antitank rocket penetrated at the left front of the tank near the driver and away from the commander. It should be noted that tank commanders often had their hatches open to assess situations since the periscopes were limited in visibility. There is the possibility that Tomasheski was still in the turret basket but not visible in the U.S. Army photo. It is also possible that he died after exiting the vehicle.

First Lt. Walter T. Anderson, Sicily, 1943. FRITZ

Sergeant Tomasheski, England, 1944. TOMASHESKI

On 7 June 1944, Company D attacked southwest of Vierville in support of 101st Airborne units. In addition to the deaths of McNally, Tomasheski, and Curry, T/5 Tadeus J. Wozny, Pvt. Ray Bonzo, and Private Hughes were wounded during the engagement. Along with the loss of Tank #12, Tank #10 was hit by a projectile that drilled a hole through the front glacis plate, but was later repaired. Company D returned to Culoville for the night. Tank #17 had not reported in since the landing. Below is an original overlay of the enemy situation on 8 June from the National Archives. This overlay would be placed on a GSGS (MI4) map from the Directorate of Military Survey, War Office, London. These maps use a special grid coordinate system, as shown in the upper left and lower right of the overlay. This overlay fits GSGS map sheet 6E/324 with a 1/50,000 scale.

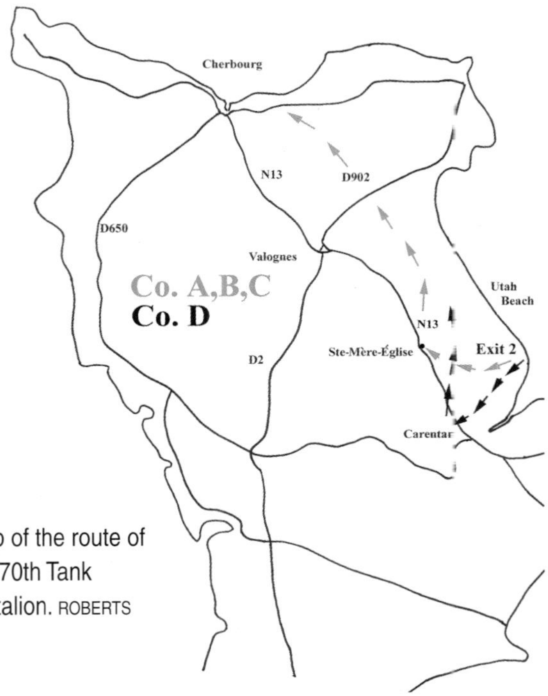

Map of the route of the 70th Tank Battalion. ROBERTS

Original overlay to the right of the enemy situation on 8 June 1944, from the National Archives. ROBERTS

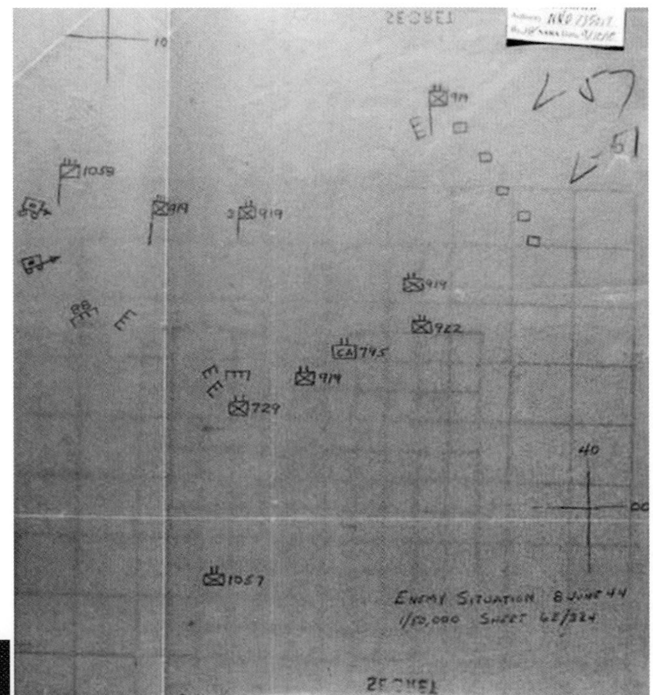

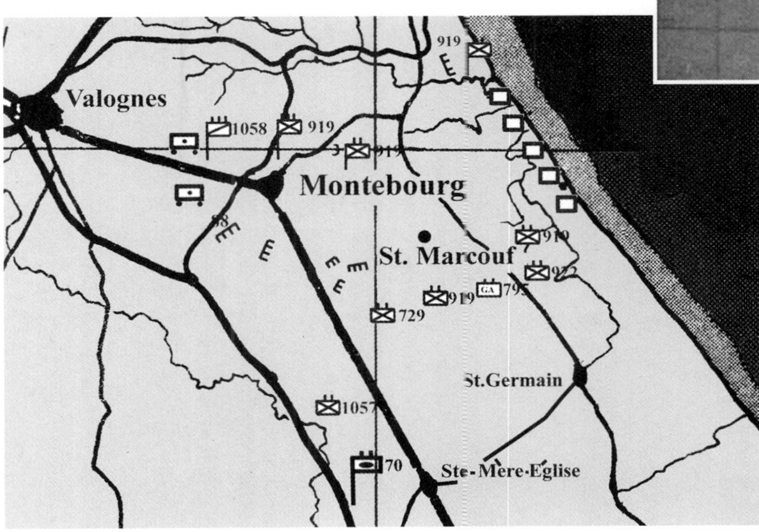

This map is a GSGS map showing the information from the overlay and the 70th command post. There were other Allied units in the area that are not annotated on the map. Some of the German units include the Grenadier-Regiment 919, the 3rd Battalion of Grenadier-Regiment 919, and the Georgian Battalion 795. ROBERTS

ON TO CHERBOURG

With the beachhead and nearby areas well established, the engagements moved from the flooded areas to hedgerow country, which again strongly favored the defenders. The hedgerows, piles of stone with hedges intertwined that separated various farm fields, were formidable obstacles and slowed the Allied advance. Tanks were forced to drive up and over them, with a high probability of getting stuck.

Temporary 70th camp near a hedgerow. ERICKSON

15 June/44	Utah Beach	Normandy, France
16 June/44	Reunion Camp	St. Mere Eglise, France
20 June/44	Papachute Camp	Joganville, France
21 June/44	Camp Carrado	Montebourg, France
22 June/44	Camp Barrows	Valognes, France
1 July/44	Jerry Camp	Orglandes, France
8 July/44	Camp Roccio	Houteville, France
12 July/44	Camp Williams	Auvers, France
22 July/44	Gas Alarm Camp	Segueville, France

70th camps at Normandy. TAYNTON

On 7 June, Companies A and B moved with the 8th Infantry Regiment of the 4th Infantry Division in an attack on Ste-Mère-Église. The companies engaged the enemy about a thousand yards south of town and linked up with the 82nd Airborne Division at Ste-Mère-Église at about 1445 hours with heavy enemy resistance. The 505th Parachute Infantry Regiment had captured the town on D-Day. The companies moved to the north side of the city to form a defensive perimeter for the evening.

Sgt. Ralph Erickson was a member of Headquarters Company, 70th Tank Battalion, and took several photos on approximately D-Day+1 of wrecked armor on Highway N13. This photo, taken by him, is of a German Sturmgeschütz III (StuG III) knocked out on Highway N13 just north of Ste-Mère-Église. The StuG III was a formidable assault gun that was often encountered by the 70th.

Soldiers spent 7 June mopping up pockets of enemy resistance near the beachhead and causeways leaving the beachhead. The 8th Infantry Regiment, supported by the 70th, attacked and captured enemy forces in Écoquenéauville and then relieved the 82nd Airborne in Ste-Mère-Église. The attack continued and forced the enemy west of the Montebourg Highway with over 300 German soldiers killed and 174 taken prisoner.

A knocked-out Sturmgeschütz (StuG) III that supported Grenadier-Regiment 1058 in a counterattack on paratroopers in Ste-Mère-Église. This appears to be on the road to Montebourg outside the town. The vehicle was knocked out by a 57mm antitank gun of the 80th Airborne Antiaircraft Battalion. The vehicle belonged to the commander of Sturmgeschütz-Abteilung 1243. ERICKSON

Knocked-out Sherman M4 at the right with a knocked-out German Marder 3, Ausf. M, from Panzerjäger-Abteilung 243 (1st Company) in the distance on the highway, also north of Ste-Mère-Église. The Sherman tank rolled over on its left side (foreground) is most likely the tank commanded by 2nd Lt. Thomas J. Tighe. ERICKSON

Russian 15.2cm KH433/l(r) gun, pressed into service by the Germans, captured near Ste-Mère-Église. ERICKSON

A 75mm PaK 40 L/48 Auf. Gw Lorraine Schlepper (Marder 1). It was common for the Germans to use captured vehicles as platforms for self-propelled guns. In this photo, the chassis is French and the upper structure and gun are German. This vehicle was used by the Panzerjäger-Abteilung 709. ERICKSON

German prisoners marching off to the POW camp near Ste-Mère-Église, June 1944. ERICKSON

On 8 June, Companies A, B, and C left Ste-Mère-Église at 1600 hours, advanced in line formation, and engaged enemy positions near Azeville at 1730 hours in support of the 22nd Infantry Regiment. Companies A, B, and C disengaged from the fight and returned to the assembly area at 2200 hours. Lieutenant Songer and PFC Joseph R. Rayner were slightly wounded in action. Tanks #1 and #3 of Company B received direct hits from "88s."

On 10 and 11 June, the battalion attacked objectives southwest of Montebourg on the way to Cherbourg. From 12 to 19 June, they cleaned up pockets of enemy resistance and traveled through Montebourg and Valognes. Each of these towns was nearly destroyed during bombing and fighting. The enemy was ordered to hold Cherbourg at all costs, which explained the heavy resistance encountered on the way to that city. On 28 June, Cherbourg fell to the Allied advance, with many German prisoners taken.

From June 12 to 19, the 70th engaged enemy forces in Quineville. Heavy bombing and Allied engagements virtually destroyed Montebourg. The battalion then attacked northeast through Valognes, another city reduced to ruins.

Azeville battery casemate #3. This photo was taken by Capt. Lewis Taynton of the 70th Tank Battalion sometime after 15 June 1944, when he arrived at Utah Beach with the 70th Tank Battalion Service Company. Note the painted camouflage on the concrete. This fortification was used as indirect fire since it required a forward observer to direct and correct firing on enemy forces. These casemates were constructed in 1942 and upgraded by Field Marshal Erwin Rommel in 1944. TAYNTON

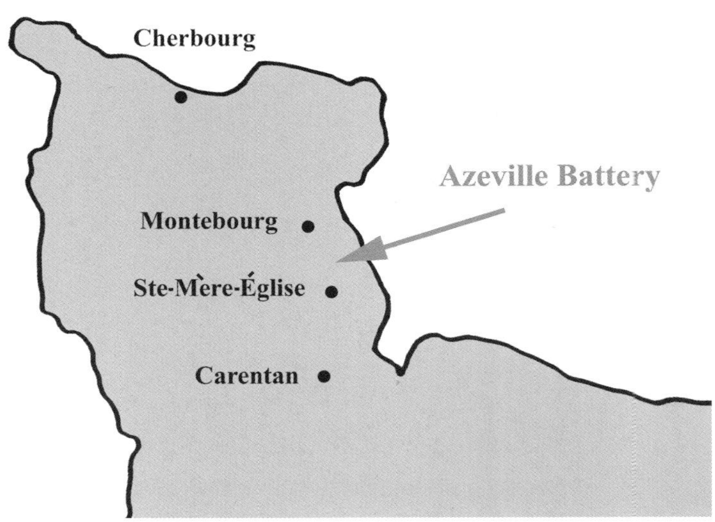

Map showing approximate location of the Azeville battery. ROBERTS

Captain Bushey of the 70th Tank Battalion with a captured German vehicle originally owned by the commander of the Cherbourg garrison. ERICKSON

Captured Schwimmwagen named *Heil*. ERICKSON

Tank B16 traveling through Valognes in June 1944. NATIONAL ARCHIVES

Catholic church of St.-Malo in Valognes, France, in ruins after the Allied bombardment. Sergeant Erickson took this picture in June 1944 while the 70th traveled through the city. ERICKSON

Bulldozer clearing cebris in a town. ERICKSON

LST 290 unloads on or after 15 June 1944. ERICKSON

Heading toward Utah Beach on an LST. This is probably Service Company of the 70th Tank Battalion, which arrived at Utah Beach on approximately 15 June 1944. The LST is loaded with ammunition and supply trucks. U.S. ARMY

DUKW (pronounced "duck") being launched from an LST, Utah Beach, June 1944. ERICKSON

Headquarters Company personnel unloading a trailer from an LST, Utah Beach, June 1944. ERICKSON

LCT 475 sailing by an LST carrying 70th Headquarters Company personnel and equipment. ERICKSON

Radio operator at the command post in Normandy along with a situation map. ERICKSON

Commanders meeting at a command post with a situation map, somewhere in hedgerow country, Normandy. ERICKSON

A 70th DD tank moving up to attack enemy positions in hedgerow country, Normandy. ERICKSON

German graves in Normandy. TAYNTON

A 70th Tank Battalion WC-57 command car and trailer from Headquarters Company in hedgerow country. ERICKSON

Captain Taynton at Battery Hamburg, casemate #3 (Turm 3). TAYNTON

Toward the end of June the 70th attacked Cherbourg, which was captured on 28 June. Captain Taynton visited the Cherbourg area and took photos of Battery Hamburg, a formidable fortification just to the east of Cherbourg that was firing on U.S. ships bringing supplies to the various landing beaches. In the above photo, the weapon appears to be a naval gun, as evidenced by the characteristic turret and armor design (24cm SK L/40 naval gun used on 1890 vintage German and Austro-Hungarian cruisers).

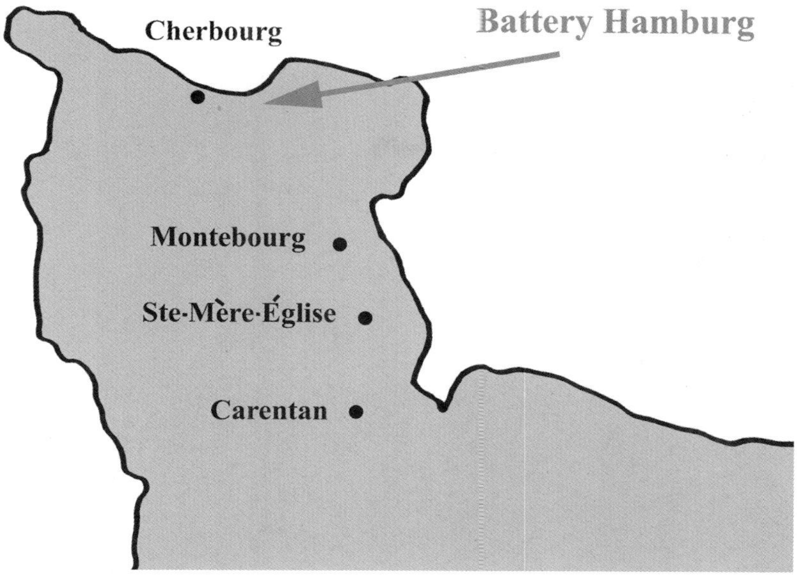

Approximate location of Battery Hamburg in France. ROBERTS

Captain Taynton at Battery Hamburg, casemate #2 (Turm 2). The photo attests to the size of these guns. The guns of Battery Hamburg fired on Operation Overlord battleships, scoring two hits on the USS *Texas* BB-35. Luckily, the ammunition used did not explode, limiting the damage to the ship. Here, Captain Taynton is holding the electric controls that operate the traverse and elevation system of the gun. TAYNTON

An 88mm antiaircraft gun used against ground targets. Several of these weapons were used throughout Normandy to the detriment of the American armor. TAYNTON

As Company A approached the coast near Cherbourg, the lead tank was taken under fire by five German E-boats. The company withdrew to protected positions and fired at the E-boats. Allied air support was notified of the location of the enemy vessels, and within fifteen minutes, aircraft attacked and drove off the Germans. However, while near V-1 launching sites at Cherbourg, the battalion was mistakenly bombed by Allied aircraft, a common problem with quick advances and rapid enemy withdrawal.

During the Normandy Campaign, twenty-nine 70th soldiers were killed in action, thirty-one were listed as missing, forty-eight were wounded, and thirty-two tanks were lost with some salvaged and repaired.

CARENTAN–PERIERS

The 70th then turned southwest on 6 July toward Periers, with Company B supporting the 12th Infantry Regiment and Company A in support of the 8th Infantry Regiment. The terrain included nearly impenetrable hedgerows, resulting in slow progress. The attack toward Periers was a slugfest in support of the 4th Division and required all available tanks from the battalion.

Company B lost four tanks on 7 July, and in the following days up until the fall of Periers, all remaining tanks were in action supporting the 4th Infantry Division. The enemy resisted with everything they had, including mines, mortars, small arms, machine guns, artillery, and tanks.

For a short period of time (16–18 July), the 70th was attached to the 83rd Infantry Division. On 17 July while bivouacked near Culot, a gas attack false alarm occurred, during which all 70th members struggled to put on gas masks.

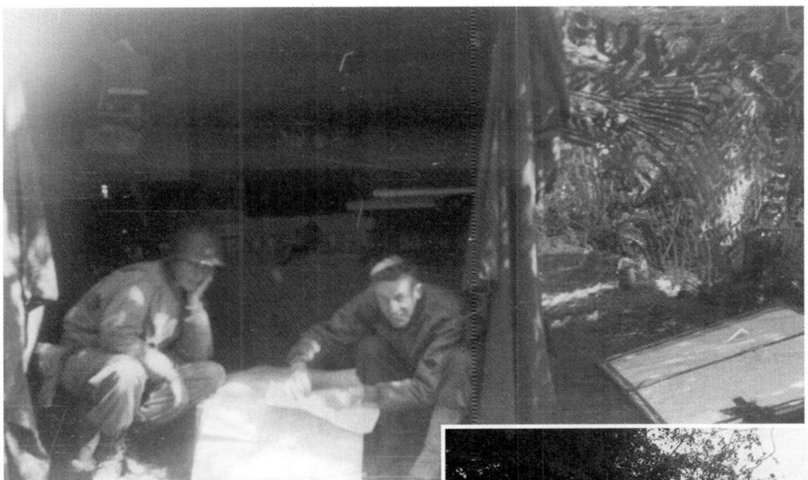

Reviewing situation maps at Headquarters Company. ERICKSON

Panzer III Ausf. G, Normandy, early July 1944. TAYNTON

Captain Taynton in front of an Sd.Kfz. 7 prime mover with a Panzer III Ausf. G in the background, early July 1944. TAYNTON

Panzer IV Ausf. J of the 2nd SS Panzer Division "Das Reich." This vehicle is from 5th Company, 2nd Platoon, Vehicle #3, July 1944. TAYNTON

German 88mm gun. TAYNTON

Panzer V Ausf. A "Panther" of "Das Reich," 2nd SS Panzer Division, near Sainteny. TAYNTON

Sherman M4A1 opposing a Panther with multiple hits from the 75mm high-velocity gun of the Panzer V. There also appear to be hits from handheld antitank weapons. TAYNTON

Side view of the Sherman M4A1 tank. TAYNTON

Company B diary photo. This is a Panzer V from "Das Reich" near Sainteny, France, July 1944. NATIONAL ARCHIVES

Panzer V "Panther" Ausf. A of 2nd SS Panzer Division "Das Reich" near Sainteny, July 1944. TAYNTON

Two Panzer V Ausf. A "Panther" tanks in a collection yard in Normandy in late July 1944. Both vehicles, belonging to Panzer-Lehr, were lost during a failed counterattack on 11 July. ERICKSON

Photo of a Sturmgeschütz (StuG) IV, July 1944, located in one of the collection yards. This vehicle belonged to the 17th SS Panzergrenadier Division "Götz von Berlichingen." This unit was the only German unit in Normandy equipped with StuG IVs at that time. TAYNTON

Photo of Captain Taynton on an Sd.Kfz. 9 prime mover, early July 1944. TAYNTON

Panzer V Ausf. A "Panther" named *Ursala* of Panzer Lehr—knocked out on 11 July 1944—in a collection yard, Normandy, late July 1944. Captain Taynton is seated on the turret at the left. TAYNTON

MOVING TOWARD ST. LÔ

On 25 July, the 70th supported three infantry battalions along the St. Lô–Periers Road. The objective was to take the highway and attack south of Marigny, which was achieved despite heavy resistance in the form of artillery and mortar fire. Casualties were heavy, and replacements arrived in numbers higher than normal. New men were given a short orientation and immediately put into tanks that rolled out for the next battle. At least one dozer tank each day was knocked out. The Allies had air superiority during the day, but at night German aircraft appeared overhead, dropping bombs.

Campus Red Forward, command post, 70th Tank Battalion. ERICKSON

Captain Taynton on a German 3.7cm flak gun mount. TAYNTON

Shortly after D-Day, Command determined that Allied armored vehicles were not as well camouflaged as that of the enemy. A test was performed to observe how camouflage could be improved. C Company tank *Columbia Lou* (C15) was used as a test rig to prove the concept. Sommerfeld netting was placed around the tank so that tree branches could be inserted to camouflage the vehicle. Command felt this was an effective method, and it was adopted by many Allied armored units.

During this period, Sgt. Curtis Cullen of the 102nd Cavalry Squadron developed a hedgerow cutter that attached to the front of Allied tanks. This device allowed tanks to quickly blast through the hedgerows without having to climb up and over the obstacles, which would expose the vulnerable underbody to enemy fire. Many tanks were fitted with hedgerow cutters for the launch of Operation Cobra. Sergeant Cullen received the Legion of Merit for this development. Relatively few 70th tanks were equipped with the Cullen device—the dozer tanks of the 70th worked as well or better.

M4 *Columbia Lou* with netting applied (left) and tree branches installed (right). TAYNTON

T/4 Ross on a D Company tank equipped with a Cullen hedgerow cutter. ROSS

Front glacis plate of a medium tank from the 746th Tank Battalion showing projectile penetrations that probably disabled the vehicle.
TAYNTON

Maj. Gen. Raymond O. Barton, commanding general of the 4th Infantry Division, presenting a decoration for valor to Lt. Carlisle Ring and other members of the 70th in France, July 1944. From left to right: Maj. Henry Davidson, Capt. Gordon Brodie (one of four Silver Stars he received), Lt. Richard Bauer, and Lt. John Townsend.
BRODIE

CHAPTER 6

Northern France–Belgium

ST. LÔ

With the capture of Cherbourg and consolidation of enemy positions on the Cotentin Peninsula, Allied forces of the First Army were poised along a front near the French town of St. Lô. The plan was for the First Army to punch a hole in the German lines, allowing the Third Army (Patton) to travel through in a long sweeping flank movement across the favorable tank country of northern France. The strategy was to encircle enemy forces, cut off their supply routes, and destroy or capture as many enemy units as possible.

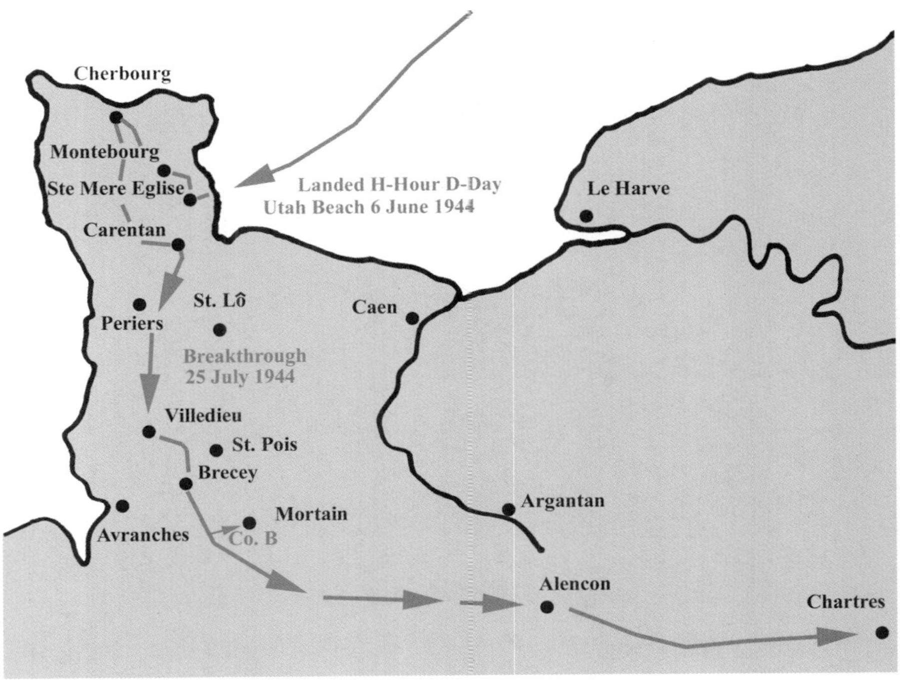

Normandy to Paris. ROBERTS

On 26 July 1944, Companies A, B, and C of the 70th supported the 8th Infantry Division near St. Lô after a heavy air attack on the town by Allied aircraft. The actual targets destroyed were fewer than anticipated, but the intensity of the bombing demoralized and confused the enemy so much that they began to retreat. German armor could not move freely without being attacked by aircraft, which helped the 70th move more readily toward objectives. The vast number of Allied aircraft sorties had the undesirable effect of accidental bombing of the 70th near St. Lô after the battalion had been obscured by smoke from previous bombings. Casualties were sustained by the 70th and 8th Infantry Regiment, along with vehicles hit.

Despite all the confusion they pressed forward against significant enemy resistance, transforming the town of St. Lô and its countryside into a wasteland. Birds and animals lay dead in the fields along with burned-out hulks of vehicles. Bomb craters altered the agrarian countryside. The movement forward toward the St. Lô–Periers Road became a more rapid indication that the Germans were stunned and disorganized, with the province of Brittany open for the taking. On 1 August, the Third Army attacked through the sector, capturing Granville and Avranches, beginning its sweep into Brittany, and initiating the famed "Patton dash across France."

Patton reveled in headlines, and this operation fit the bill. Admiration goes to the 70th and those units who slugged it out with the enemy to make the breakout possible. While the Third Army was attacking across France, the 70th moved southeast toward Villedieu les Poeles, Brecey, and Mortain, supporting the 4th Infantry Division. Company A was attached to the 8th Infantry Regiment of the 4th, Company B to the 12th Infantry Regiment, and Company C to the 22nd Infantry Regiment. Company D acted as a screening force. B Company attacked Villedieu and encountered stiff enemy resistance.

Photo of M4 medium tank traveling through a nearly destroyed town in France. It should be noted that church steeples were often destroyed preemptively since snipers were usually hiding within. 70TH HISTORY

23 July/44	Break Through Camp	Les Frenes, France
28 July/44	Air Raid Camp	La Lievrerie, France
30 July/44	Camp Brown	Pont Brocard, France
3 Aug/44	Camp Reims	La Bloutiere, France
6 Aug/44	Ammunition Camp	La Pinelliers, France
9 Aug/44	Childrens Camp	St. Laurent De Cueves, France
11 Aug/44	Swimming hole Camp	Buais, France
18 Aug/44	Camp Argentan	La Paguerie, France
24 Aug/44	Lost Camp	Dampierre, France
28 Aug/44	Camp Paris	Saint Mande Park, Paris, France
29 Aug/44	Camp Welborn	Clichy, Paris, France
31 Aug/44	Out Post Camp	Pondron, France
3 Sept/44	City Park Camp	Saint Quentin, France
6 Sept/44	German Camp	La Patte D'Oie, France
11 Sept/44	Camp St. Mihiel	St. Hubert, Belgium
12 Sept/44	Flame Thrower Camp	Bovigny, Belgium
15 Sept/44	Camp St. Vith	St. Vith. Belgium

Camps for the 70th from 23 July to 15 September 1944. TAYNTON

Traveling through a devastated city in France. The vertical piece of metal to the right is a makeshift device to protect against piano-wire booby traps strung across the streets by the retreating enemy. The piano wire could decapitate an unsuspecting driver or passenger. ERICKSON

Dozer clears away a barricade put up by the enemy in a town. ERICKSON

The attack progressed toward St. Pois, and the north bank of the See River was taken by the 8th Infantry Regiment supported by Company A. Companies B and C slugged their way to objectives north of St. Pois under heavy tank and artillery fire from the enemy. In early August, the battalion was cleaning up pockets of enemy resistance with no personnel and equipment lost. Shortly thereafter, the Germans prepared a counterattack to cut off the Third Army near the towns of Mortain and Avranches. Company B and Combat Team 12 moved to Mortain in anticipation of the counteroffensive. Company A and the rest of the battalion remained with Combat Team 8 as a reserve force. Company A had just received the new up-gunned medium tanks with the 76mm gun. The new gun was an improvement over the standard 75mm, as it had higher-velocity ammunition and more penetrating power. Still, it could not defeat enemy tanks in a frontal assault at distance, to the consternation of 70th tankers and the higher-ups at Supreme Headquarters Allied Expeditionary Force (SHAEF). An attack on an enemy tank usually was initiated from the side, since the armor there was considerably less thick.

The battle for Mortain was fierce, as the Germans tried to push the Allies back toward the sea. In the three days of 9–11 August, the 70th—along with the 12th and 22nd Infantry Regiments—held the line, thwarting the attack that eventually fizzled, initiating the enemy retrograde toward the German border (Siegfried Line). Headquarters, Service, and D Companies were now camped 8 miles southeast of Le Teilleul, located south of the Mortain–Domfront Highway. Service Company was now commanded by Capt. Thomas E. Barbour. The never-ending search for spare parts continued, and soldiers from Service Company would often travel to supply depots to get badly needed items for the tanks, half-tracks, and trucks. Because of the rapid Allied advance through France, supply units had trouble keeping up. Spare parts were in short supply and required a division-level requisition. Many times the 70th maintenance personnel were turned away because the 70th was merely a battalion, not a division. It did not take long for Service Company personnel to learn that in order to get spares, they had to call themselves the 70th Division and provide a case of liquor.

Service Company personnel replacing radial engines in a medium tank. The wrecker was typically used to hoist engines out of the tank onto a repair stand. Usually the damaged engines were sent back to ordnance for repair, but some repairs were made in the field. ISAACS

Claude Haury, a member of Service Company, in a town in Northern France, summer 1944. ISAACS

Service Company working on a radial engine, summer 1944. Early M4 medium tanks had radial engines, while later versions had the GAA Ford V8 engine. ISAACS

Graves of two German soldiers. Karl Paul is the full name of the soldier buried on the left. Emil Neumann (the soldier buried on the right) had his unit listed as K P Pion.Btl.271, i.e., the engineer battalion of 271 Infantry Division, which in June 1944 was still on its way to the front. Obergefreiter Emil Neumann, who was killed on 27 June 1944 and is now in Orglandes cemetery, was thirty-nine years old. TAYNTON

German Mark V Panther disabled and abandoned on D-44 (Rue de St.-Malo) outside Coutances, France, in July 1944. Panther tanks were formidable weapons but could be defeated by a side or rear shot from an M4 medium tank. ROBERTS

Tank-engine repair crew from Service Company in front of a wrecker used to change out tank engines, summer 1944. ISAACS

Paul Duda, Company B jeep driver. DIXON

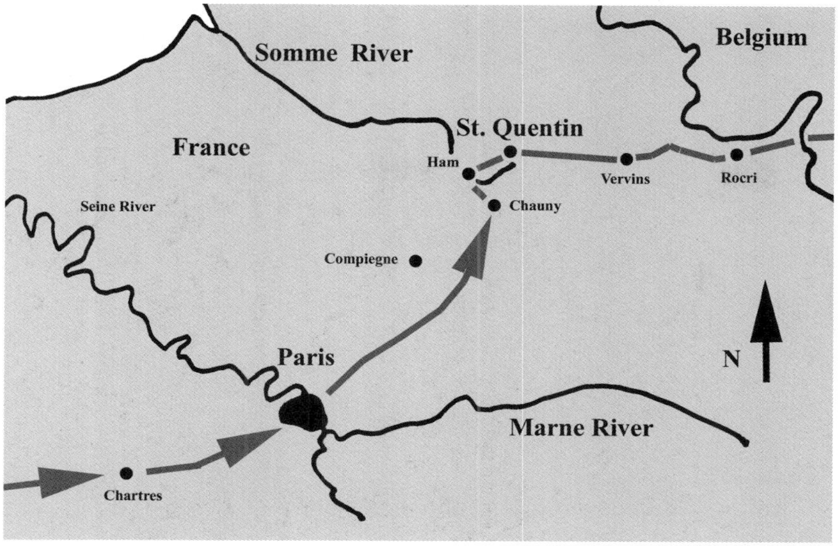

Map of the route of the 70th from Chartres, through Paris, and on to St. Quentin, summer 1944. ROBERTS

Lieutenant Colonel Welborn receiving the Distinguished Service Cross. Gen. Lawton Collins, commander of VII Corps, is standing second from the left in the foreground. TAYNTON

Disabled M4 tank with Captain Taynton on the right. The track has become detached. Northern France, 1944. TAYNTON

This USO show in the summer of 1944 was a real treat for the tankers of the 70th, giving them a break in the tensions of tank warfare. Note the stage is a flatbed trailer used to transport tanks. ERICKSON

A singer entertaining the troops at a USO show in northern France, summer 1944. ERICKSON

Pedi-cab in Paris, summer 1944. TAYNTON

American Red Cross office in Paris, summer 1944. TAYNTON

PARIS

Mid-August days were uneventful, but night attacks by enemy aircraft were common. Bombs the size of 40mm mortar shells rained down on the 70th, resulting in casualties and the destruction of the kitchen unit of Company C. On 17 August, the battalion moved to a location midway between Pré-en-Pail and Carrouges where units of the French Army were encamped. From 11 to 23 August, the battalion performed maintenance but kept in contact with the enemy as they retreated rapidly toward Germany. The 70th traveled through St. Pois, St.-Laurent-de-Cuves, La Chappelle-Cécelin, Brecy, St. Hilaire-du-Harcouët, and Montigny with little enemy opposition. The townsfolk always came out to wave American flags and celebrate their liberation.

Because of the rapid advance, convoys often drove through the night, and tank drivers became hypnotized while watching the small taillight of the vehicle in front. Military vehicles had two sets of lights, one for normal driving and a small one for combat mode to avoid detection. The taillight slits were often called "cat eyes." On 24 August, the battalion was in the vicinity of St. Yon, 20 miles south of Paris. Company A was at Villemoisson, Company B at Bois de Vincennes, Company C at Longjumeau, and Company D at St. Yon.

Captain Taynton of Service Company sitting on the bumper of his jeep on the Champs-Élysées with the Arc de Triomphe in the background. The bumper reads "1st Army 70th Armor." TAYNTON

Captain Taynton on leave in Paris in Class A uniform, standing in front of the Arc de Triomphe, August 1944. TAYNTON

Lt. Edgar C. Heist of Company D in Paris, 26 August 1944. He is pictured with one of many women who welcomed the tankers as they repatriated the city. The 70th was the first American armor to enter Paris. TAYNTON

Edward C. Provaznik (left) and Sgt. Daniel E. Knorr, Europe, 1944. JENSEN

Crewmen Paul W. Gaul, Provaznik, and George F. Hammersmith, Europe, 1944. JENSEN

Eiffel Tower. TAYNTON

Eiffel Tower and several 70th officers on leave, August 1944. CONNORS

Notre Dame, August 1944. TAYNTON

Eternal flame at the Arc de Triomphe, August 1944. TAYNTON

William H. Jones, Francis F. Ross, Thomas J. Hale, and William P. Thomas at Paris encampment, standing in front of a half-track, probably from Headquarters Company, northern France, summer 1944. ROSS

T/5 Ross. ROSS

Central Registration Bureau, Paris, where all personnel on leave had to report, August 1944. TAYNTON

Opera house in Paris, August 1944. TAYNTON

70th Tank Battalion camp in Paris, summer 1944. Fencing was set up to reduce theft, since shortages of fuel and food existed. ERICKSON

Major Davidson at the Paris camp, summer 1944. ERICKSON

Volleyball game during respite in Paris, summer 1944. ERICKSON

Residents of the Paris area were often quite thankful for the liberation from the Germans and congregated around the camp, summer 1944. ERICKSON

70th Tank Battalion Medical Detachment members receiving awards, summer 1944. ERICKSON

Award presentation, summer 1944. ERICKSON

Kneeling: Dr. Isadore Shechner. First row, left: Barbour. First row, far right: Lieutenant Colonel Welborn. Back row, second from left: Frank Anderson. Back row, third from left: Raiforth Blackstone. Summer 1944. ERICKSON

Reviewing maps and map overlays. ERICKSON

From left to right: Captain Barbour, Captain Taynton, and Warrant Officer Arrington B. Turner. TURNER

Medical detachment formation, Paris, summer 1944. ERICKSON

Battalion formation and parade, Paris, summer 1944. ERICKSON

Wreckage of a German plane in a field. TAYNTON

A 70th crewmember in Paris. TAYNTON

Captain Taynton reviewing maps, summer 1944. TAYNTON

Sergeant Vassey on the left at camp near Paris, summer 1944. ERICKSON

Lieutenant Colonel Welborn having a cup of coffee with the troops, summer 1944. ERICKSON

L-4 observation aircraft in a field. TAYNTON

Company D, under the command of Capt. Herman Finklestein, was ordered to support the 12th Infantry Regiment under the command of Colonel Luckett as it moved into Paris. The unit entered the city through Longjumeau, Athis-Mons, Villejuif, Gentilly, by the destroyed Renault Factory to Porte d'Italie, which was the bivouac area. The French civilians were jubilant and celebrated most of the day, to the point that a fence had to be set up to keep them out of the camp where repair work on tanks and other equipment was taking place. Occasionally, French resistance groups (Free French of the Interior, FFI) would pass by and request gasoline so they could ferret out the remaining Germans.

Reprisals against suspected German collaborators started to occur, as mobs singled out individuals for "justice." Typically a person who was thought to have been friendly with the Germans was tried, convicted, sentenced, and punished on the spot. The punishment was shaving the head, stripping, and painting with tar. Of course this treatment was repulsive to the soldiers of the 70th, but they were under orders not to interfere. The FFI were helpful, however, in keeping order around the 70th camp and preventing theft of food and equipment.

One day, when an attempt was made to assassinate General de Gaulle, a platoon from the 70th was ordered into the heart of the city to quell sporadic firing. The platoon paraded through town under the command of Sgt. Ray T. Hart and returned shortly afterward.

There were additional engagements of the 70th with the Germans at the northeast perimeter of the city, resulting in casualties. On 27 August, Company A moved to the vicinity of Montfermeil, and Company C to the vicinity of Clichy-Sur-Bois, with Company B between Companies A and C. On 28 August, Company D moved to the forest of Vincennes between Companies A and C. This movement was in pursuit of the enemy northeast of Paris, and the companies encountered stiff resistance. Four tanks from Company A, one from Company B, and two from Company C were lost.

This person was accused of collaborating with the Germans. Accused collaborators' heads were shaved, and then they were stripped, tarred, and paraded through the street. Allied units were ordered not to interfere with these proceedings. ERICKSON

MOVING ON TO NORTHEASTERN FRANCE

On 29 August, the battalion as a whole unit (for the second time since Sicily) was ordered to seize the ground 2,000 yards south of Tremblay Les Gonesse and hold until relieved by Combat Team 22. Companies B and C led the assault, Company A was in support, and Company D was a screening force on the left flank. The line of debarkation was 9,000 yards southeast of the objective. Company D advanced toward Roissy-en-France and captured a platoon-sized unit of Germans. The Germans were stripped of their equipment and loaded onto trucks to be sent back to the POW camp. After the battalion seized the objective, they took approximately 300 prisoners and destroyed an enemy tank along with three antitank guns.

This photo was taken by Ms. Gouget on 30 August 1944 as Tank D2 (M5A1 light tank) of Company D entered the town of Roissy-en-France, possibly on the Rue de Paris, August 1944, after capturing a platoon of German soldiers. As with many towns in France that were liberated, the townspeople appeared en masse to thank the Allied columns moving through. GOUGET/DIXON

While in the vicinity of Livry Gargan, a significant change in command occurred. Lieutenant Colonel Welborn, who had been with the battalion since the days of training at Fort Bragg, was transferred to the 3rd Armored Division. The battalion executive officer, Maj. Henry Davidson, who had also been with the 70th since Fort Bragg, became its new commander.

Lt. Col. "Jack" Welborn was admired by the men of the 70th because he always led in battle. He was promoted to full colonel and placed in command of the 33rd Armored Regiment, a unit that distinguished itself during the push into Germany.

Marne Memorial on Hill 204, summer 1944, overlooking the World War I battlefield where many American casualties occurred during the Battle of Bellau Wood. The memorial and cemetery on 42 acres is located in Belleau, northern France. Casualties from the World War I battle of Chateau Thierry are also buried at the cemetery. TAYNTON

Tankers from the 70th sitting in front of the Marne memorial, summer 1944. TAYNTON

The Aisne-Marne American Cemetery and Chapel. TAYNTON

Edward Kosmalski, Headquarters Company, in front of his M4 Sherman. This is a photo of a rare composite-hull Sherman. The manufacturer (Chrysler) welded the front of a cast-hull Sherman to a fabricated rear. Note the weld seam at the upper left of the Joe Peckerwood painted on the hull. These were manufactured starting in 1943, but it is rare to see such a modification in Europe. ERICKSON

On 31 August the 70th moved into Pondron where V-1 "buzz bombs" were observed flying toward England. On 1 and 2 September, the battalion moved north and east toward St. Quentin and entered the city on 3 September, after encountering resistance from the retreating enemy.

The 70th had advanced from St. Lô across France to St. Quentin in approximately thirty days. The 70th, attached to the 4th Infantry Division of V Corps, pushed through the city toward the Meuse River and crossed it in the vicinity of Rocroi, entering Belgium on 11 September and cutting off large units of Germans as they fled to the Siegfried Line. From 6 through 10 September, the battalion performed maintenance on vehicles and struggled to get replacement parts, ammunition, and fuel, since the rapid advance had outpaced supply lines. They received four flamethrower tanks for the assault on the Siegfried Line. On 11 September, the battalion moved through St. Hubert, Boyigny, and camped in a large forest 1.5 miles from Winterscheid, Germany.

Headquarters Company, 1st Platoon, Tank #2 (M4), summer 1944. This is the same tank (*Cannon Ball*) that was swamped in chapter 5 (see page 128). Here it has been recovered and reused. Note the white star has been rubbed out since it was easily seen by German gunners. ERICKSON

From left to right: Captain Bushey, Captain Taynton, Major Davidson, and Lieutenant Colonel Welborn. DIXON

John Malatesta in Belgium next to his M4 medium tank named *Blondie*, August 1944. MALATESTA

A T/5 enlisted man sits on a jeep, 1944. ERICKSON

Several photos in which flame-thrower tanks are being tested. The E4-5 flamethrower was installed on four of the 70th tanks for evaluation purposes on 11 September 1944. The 70th was equipped with flamethrowers in anticipation of an assault on the Siegfried Line. These are M4A1 76mm tanks. TAYNTON

Crossing the Maas or Meuse River near Fumay, France. ERICKSON

Destroyed bridge over the Meuse River at the left and pontoon bridge at the right, Fumay, France, September 1944. ERICKSON

Pontoon bridge over the Meuse River at Fumay, France, September 1944. ERICKSON

T2 tank retriever *Crazy Crate* of Company C recovering a disabled dozer tank. ERICKSON

Flail tank (crab) used to clear mines. The rotating chains on the front of the Sherman had steel balls at the ends and would strike the ground repeatedly, setting off the mines. CONNORS

A T1E3 "Aunt Jemima" mine-clearing tank attachment, used primarily with the Sherman, with large disk-shaped wheels that would sink into the ground and set off mines, October 1944. CONNORS

Captain Taynton sitting at the tail of an FW 190 German fighter aircraft, August 1944. TAYNTON

German bomb with incendiary bomblets that released once the bomb was dropped from an aircraft. TAYNTON

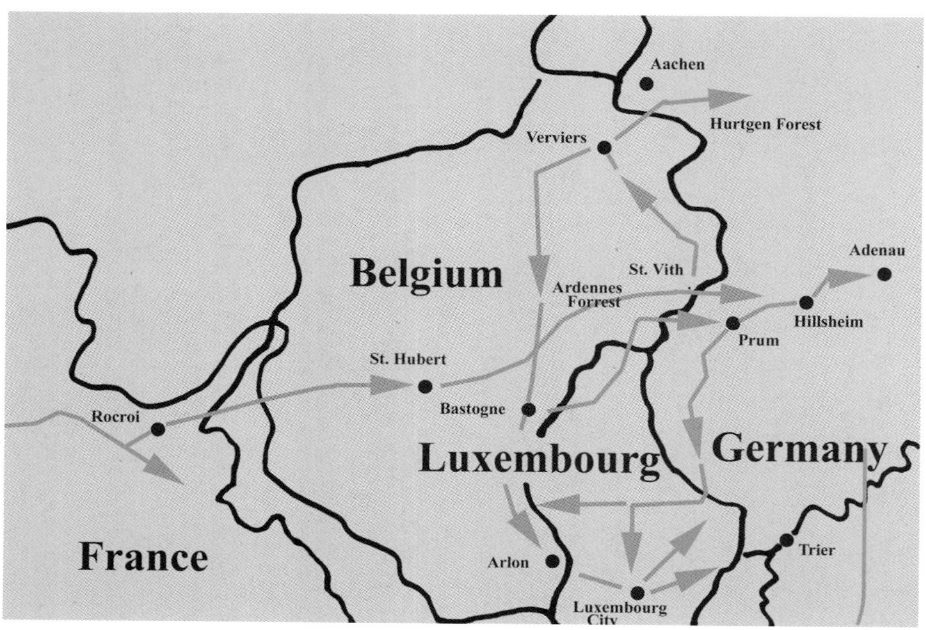

Route of the 70th from northern France through Belgium and into Germany in 1944. ROBERTS

Captain Taynton (left) in front of a German monument. TAYNTON

Destroyed German Sd.Kfz. 251 half-tracks. ERICKSON

Tank crew in an M4 medium tank. ERICKSON

Company B, Tank #12, an M4A1 75mm medium tank with cast hull, in a field in northern France, 1944. DIXON

Disabled M4 medium tank. The front drive sprocket and track sections are blown away, possibly from an antitank mine or antitank gun. ISAACS

LUXEMBOURG, BELGIUM

Two boys playing around a destroyed Sd.Kfz. 250 German half-track in Belgium. TAYNTON

Camp in Belgium, September 1944. TAYNTON

Photo of an M4 75mm with composite hull, Luxembourg, December 1944. The front of the hull was cast metal while the rear was welded, a rare construction; very few were manufactured in this manner. Captain Taynton is in front. TAYNTON

German prisoners on the way to a POW camp, Luxembourg 1944. These were the lucky ones, as their treatment by the Americans was better than that by the Russians. TAYNTON

Camp in Belgium using commandeered material, fall 1944. TAYNTON

Captain Taynton in Belgium, fall 1944. TAYNTON

From left to right: Edward Gossler, William Winters (platoon sergeant), Clarence Jay, Clarence Kleinhuizen, and Tom Young. Luxembourg, December 1944. KNOEBEL

Tank commander Clarence Jay in front of his M4A3 76mm tank, Luxembourg, December 1944. KNOEBEL

From left to right: Robert Knoebel, Edgar Morrison (loader), Albert Lennex, and Darell Banks, Luxembourg, December 1944. KNOEBEL

Back row (left to right): Tom Young, Clarence Jay, Clarence Kleinhuizen, and Eugene Mayberry. Front row (left to right): Edward Gossler and Edgar Morrison (loader). Luxembourg, 1944. KNOEBEL

CHAPTER 7

Germany

SIEGFRIED LINE

On 13 September, Company B was the first unit of the 70th to cross into Germany, and other units followed shortly thereafter. The battalion command post was established northwest of the town of Winterscheid. Company C, supporting the 1st Battalion, 22nd Infantry Regiment, attacked the Siegfried Line using armor-piercing (AP) and high-explosive (HE) rounds at point-blank range, as well as flamethrower tanks. This attack knocked out machine-gun nests and other fortifications, allowing the infantry to penetrate the line in the Schnee Eifel and Schlausenbacher forests. Casualties were high in both the battalion and supporting infantry. Lt. Edward F. Oates commanded the Assault Gun Platoon, which performed admirably in support of the 38th Cavalry Squadron with accurate artillery fire on German positions. Company B sustained many casualties from enemy artillery fire in the forest, while the remaining companies survived with relatively few casualties. German artillery could be heard firing four volleys at a time in the distance, which was a signal to take cover, as the projectiles would soon be landing nearby. About 20 percent of the projectiles failed to explode, attesting to the decreased reliability of some German equipment, possibly as a result of scarce resources and unavailability of skilled labor.

View of the Siegfried Line (the white line of obstructions in the distance) and a close-up view of the obstructions as viewed from Belgium. TAYNTON

As the 70th approached the Siegfried Line, Companies B and C lost one tank each under heavy enemy artillery fire. At the end of September, the 70th fought in and around the Siegfried Line in the Schnee Forest and the Schlausenbacher Forest in the vicinity of Bleialf, Elcherath, and Buchet, Germany. Company C lost one tank near Buchet while clearing out enemy positions, and Company D lost one tank. Weather had been closing in with heavy rains, making progress very slow as the 70th and 4th Infantry Division secured a 15-mile front guarding the Schnee Eifel and Monschau sectors. Fuel shortages added to the reduction in the rate of advance. The unit moved to an area near Honsfeld, Belgium, where the new flamethrower tank was introduced and training on this weapon commenced.

On 7 October, the battalion engaged enemy forces in the vicinity of Losheuntfraken, where they encountered and destroyed several roadblocks. German forces retreated, leaving much of their equipment behind. On 11 October, the 70th moved back into Germany near Hünningen, Belgium, under bad weather conditions, making supplying the unit difficult since air drops were impossible. Enemy V-1 flying bombs could be heard overhead. Large formations of aircraft could also be heard overhead, which were most likely Allied because the smaller ones were usually German. The Allied bombing attacks were having an effect on German troop movements and supply. At the beginning of November, the 70th moved to the village of Hünningen on the German border. Most of the Nazi sympathizers had been removed from the town and those cleared could remain; but one could speculate on what happened to these people when the SS divisions overran the town during the Ardennes offensive.

The 70th continued training with the flamethrower tanks. Telephones were installed on the backs of tanks to make communication with supporting infantry easier and to make the tank commander less vulnerable to small-arms fire. On 9 November, the battalion moved to a point southwest of Zweifall, Germany, under muddy weather conditions and artillery fire.

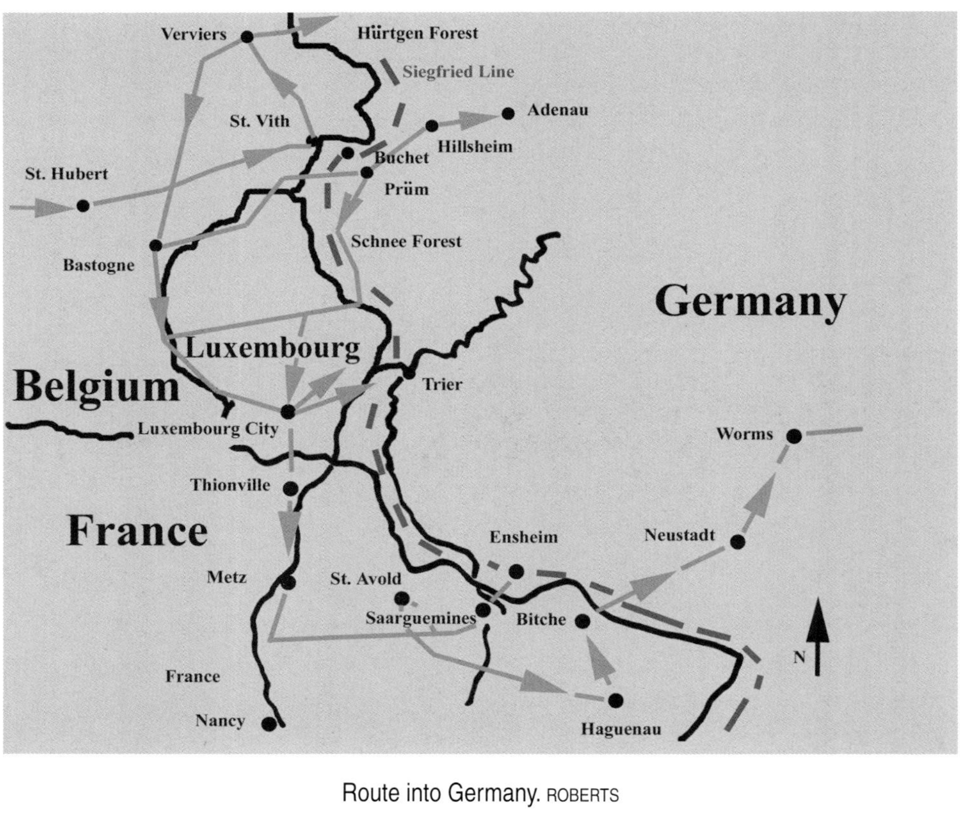

Route into Germany. ROBERTS

HÜRTGEN FOREST

From 11 to 16 November, the battalion prepared for an assault in the Hürtgen Forest. As the attack commenced, the difficulty of maneuvering tanks through the forest was realized. Some tanks threw tracks, and viewing the enemy, who may have been only a few hundred yards away in the dense forest, was difficult. Losses started to mount as the 70th began the lengthy battle. The attack on 17 November continued under difficult circumstances. The trails through the forest were narrow, with forest cover obscuring enemy positions. This was an easy area to defend with mines and antitank guns. Supporting infantry had difficulty with barbed wire, booby traps, and snipers in the woods.

From left to right: Harold C. Silverman, Frank Anderson, Harry J. McCaffrey, John H. Dixon, and Blackstone. DIXON

5 Oct/44	Buzz Bomb Alley Camp	Hepscheid, Belgium
9 Nov/44	Muddy Camp	Hergenbrath, Belgium
24 Nov/44	Nitemare Camp	Hurtgen Forest, Germany
5 Dec/44	Palace Hotel	Mondorf, Luxembourg
15 Dec/44	Luxembourg College	City of Luxembourg, Luxembourg
24 Dec/44	Luxembourg High School	City of Luxembourg, Luxembourg
28 Dec/44	Carmen Manor	City of Luxembourg, Luxembourg
17 Jan/45	Snowbound Hamlet Camp	Reuland, Luxembourg
22 Jan/45	Ghost House Bivouac	Diekirch, Luxembourg
24 Jan/45	Snowbound Hamlet Camp	Reuland, Luxembourg
28 Jan/45	Camp McKericher	Basbelline, Belgium
2 Feb/45	Cargo Camp	Burg Reuland, Belgium
4 Feb/45	Schonberg Crossroads	Schonberg, Germany
8 Feb/45	Camp Varhol	Buchet, Germany
4 Mar/45	Bombed City Camp	Prum, Germany
6 Mar/45	Task Force Camp	Schwnzheim, Germany
8 Mar/45	Rhino Camp	Honerath, Germany
9 Mar/45	Slave Labor Camp	Adenau, Germany
10 Mar/45	Task Force Camp	Schwnzheim, Germany
12 Mar/45	Overnite Camp	Mersch, Luxembourg
13 Mar/45	63rd Inf Camp	St. Jean Ruhrbach, France
14 Mar/45	Camp Hot Shot	Sarreguemines, France
16 Mar/45	Rocket Haven Camp	Ensheim, Germany
18 Mar/45	Relief Camp	Flotrange, France
20 Mar/45	Sunshine Camp	Hochfelden, France
27 Mar/45	German Staff Hotel	Wachenheim, France
29 Mar/45	Rhine River Camp	Sonderbach, Germany
30 Mar/45	Midnite Camp	Hetzbach, Germany
1 Apr/45	Jet Plane Alley	Tauberbischofshiem, Germany
3 Apr/45	Twin House Camp	Klein-Rinderfeld, Germany
8 Apr/45	Stinking hole Camp	Unter-Wittighausen, Germany
9 Apr/45	Gas Station Camp	Unter-Wittighausen, Germany
13 Apr/45	Camp Roosevelt	Schaftersheim, Germany
15 Apr/45	Camp Finklestein	Eguarhofen, Germany
18 Apr/45	Rothenberg Camp	Relchelshofen, Germany
19 Apr/45	Werewolf Camp	Bettenfeld, Germany
20 Apr/45	Camp Saville	Wornitz, Germany
21 Apr/45	Rodwell Camp	Jagstel, Germany
22 Apr/45	Camp Swink	Wasseyalfingen, Germany
23 Apr/45	Palace Camp	Aalen, Germany
24 Apr/45	Camera Camp	Giengen, Germany
25 Apr/45	Danube River Camp	Gundelfingen, Germany
26 Apr/45	River Crossing Camp	Glott, Germany
27 Apr/45	Autobahn Camp	Zusmarshausen, Germany
29 Apr/45	Augsberg, Camp	Bobingen, Germany
30 Apr/45	Camp Krach	Starnberg, Germany
7 May/45	Castle Hill Camp	Sandersdorf, Germany

Command post locations for the 70th from September 1944 through May 1945. TAYNTON

From left to right: McCaffrey, Anderson (Frank), Blackstone, and Dixon. DIXON

From left to right: Anderson (Frank), Dixon, and McCaffrey. DIXON

Clarence Kleinhuizen with captured German motorcycle, fall 1944. KLEINHUIZEN

Front row: Marvin T. Kistler and Henry W. Mills. Center top row: Manuel Freeman. Fall 1944. DIXON

M29C Weasel cargo carrier assigned to the 70th winter 1944–45. ERICKSON

M36 Jackson tank destroyer knocked out on the roadside, December 1944. It has been in this position for some time, as several field telephone wires have been laid on its turret. ERICKSON

Knocking out a German machine-gun nest with flamethrower tanks. DIXON

Service Company maintenance depot showing light and medium tanks being repaired. The wrecker was used to hoist engines in and out of the tanks. TAYNTON

The advance was slow and steady, with all companies suffering losses from antitank mines and weapons. After traveling into a clearing, the lead tank would usually be hit by antitank fire in these heavily defended areas. The dense forest restricted visibility to the extent that after one position was overrun, the next one was likely to be a few hundred yards down the road. Airbursts from artillery fire exploding at treetops rained shrapnel and wood debris down onto infantry and tankers exposed in the turrets.

On 25 November, the battalion moved south of Gressenich, Germany, and attacked enemy strongholds near Grosshau. The supporting infantry casualties were high and many tanks were knocked out. Capt. Chester W. Peterson of Company C was wounded and Captain Taynton took over command of Company C. Heavy enemy artillery and mortar fire caused the 22nd Infantry and the 70th to withdraw. On 27 November, the 70th executive officer, Robert McKericher, led a task force of two Company C tanks and tank destroyers from the 803rd Tank Destroyer Battalion in an attack on Grosshau. After several strikes on the town with many tank and infantry losses, the 70th reached its objective and moved on to the high grounds overlooking Duren. This was the breakout at the eastern edge of the Hürtgen Forest, completing one of the most brutal campaigns the 70th experienced during the war. Over this period, Captain Brodie commanded Company A, Captain Songer commanded Company B, and Captain Finkelstein commanded Company D; Captain Peterson commanded Company C until 23 November when Captain Taynton took over. Headquarters Company was commanded by Lieutenant Jones until 15 November, and then by Capt. Albert M. Krekler thereafter. Service Company was led by Captain Taynton until 24 November, and then Lt. Harold A. Oakland thereafter. The battalion commanding officer was Major Davidson, the executive officer was Maj. Robert McKericher, and the operations officer was Maj. Kenneth J. Krach.

In November, the Assault Gun Platoon under the command of Lieutenant Oates was attached to the 29th Field Artillery and provided artillery support to various advances. At the beginning of December, the 70th was camped in a heavy grove of trees in the Hürtgen Forest about two miles south of Gressenich, Germany. On 1 December, Task Force McKericher, with units from the 70th, 709th Tank Battalion, and 803rd Tank Destroyer Battalion, attacked northeast of Grosshau with the 22nd Infantry Regiment. This effort aimed to straighten the regimental line and reduce pockets of enemy resistance. Company A and 3rd Battalion, 8th Infantry Regiment, attacked in the vicinity of Haf Hardt. After the flail tank in the lead had been disabled, Sergeant Brown cleared exposed mines so that a T2 tank retriever could be brought up to haul it back. The infantry took up defensive positions until the tank assault could resume. The 2nd Platoon, Company B, moved out with the 12th Infantry Regiment to attack positions northeast of Gey, which successfully moved the line on the western edge of the town.

From 2 through 4 December, Companies B and C probed enemy positions under handheld antitank weapons fire with several tanks put out of action. On 5 December they were alerted to move, and on the seventh they traveled to Luxembourg, with the battalion camped in the new area by 11 December, ending the battle of the Hürtgen Forest. Headquarters Company was located in a schoolhouse in the city of Luxembourg, Service and A Companies in Schrassig, Company B in Scheidgen, Company C at Mondorf, and Company D in Luxembourg. The 70th had only twenty-six operational tanks, and with parts in short supply, little progress could be made on repairing damaged vehicles. Many historians would later agree that the battle of the Hürtgen Forest was a waste of men and resources.

Tank destroyers moving up with infantry. ERICKSON

ARDENNES OFFENSIVE (BATTLE OF THE BULGE)

Right after the Hürtgen Forest Campaign came the Ardennes offensive (also called the Battle of the Bulge). The 70th and 4th Infantry Division had moved back to Luxembourg. Allied infantry had taken up positions to the east and fought a delaying action as the German armor approached. The 70th spearheaded relief into Berdorf and Lauterborn and brought out Allied infantry engaged in the German onslaught. Company A and D tanks attacked Berdorf to relieve F Company of the 12th Infantry Regiment. At the same time, 3rd and 1st Platoons of Company D attacked Echternach to rescue Company E of the 12th Infantry Regiment. Company A of the 70th was assigned to open supply lines for encircled Company G, 12th Infantry Regiment, in Echternach, which was successful. Company B was assigned to open the road to Osweiler, which was successful, and L Company of the 12th Infantry Regiment was resupplied. Company B (only three tanks) was then assigned to attack enemy positions and relieve Company I, 12th Infantry Regiment, at Dickweiler, which it did by breaking up an attack by the German 212th Volksgrenadier-Division.

The Mortar Platoon set up and fired several rounds over the next two days, keeping the enemy back from a strategic valley, knocking out German ammunition and reinforcement trucks. The situation remained fluid when Allied units were cut off and freed again. Company A (1st Platoon) and Company D (3rd Platoon) tanks with infantry carried on board then attacked Berdorf to relieve Company F of the 12th Infantry Regiment. These attacks were made through the center of the towns, breaking up enemy movement and preventing the towns from falling into enemy hands. The attacks were often hampered by lack of infantry support and the problems with urban combat, including small antitank rockets.

On the afternoon of 17 December, a regimental-sized German unit was moving south from the Sauer River, and then northwest of Berdorf to Mullerthal. To counter this, 1st and 2nd Platoons of Company A, 70th, were moved to Colbert. The enemy unit changed direction and an attack was averted. It should be noted that personnel were in short supply and some tanks had two-man crews with cooks and support personnel fighting alongside them. They had difficulty observing troop movements through the fog of 18 December.

John Dixon in front of an M4A3 76mm tank, Luxembourg, winter 1944–45. DIXON

T2 tank retriever. The main 75mm gun was removed and replaced with a pipe to fool the enemy. ISAACS

Sawing firewood in the Hürtgen Forrest. From left to right: Warren J. Cameron, Gray, and Henry R. Balicki. TAYNTON

Company C was attached to Combat Team 22 along with 9th and 10th Armored Division forces and moved to Beck, Luxembourg. They arrived at the 22nd Battalion command post, but it was surrounded and the command tank was hit and knocked out. Captain Taynton transferred to another tank, pressing the attack and routing enemy forces in the area. During this action, Headquarters Company half-tracks with SCR-528 and SCR-508 radios were located near the center of the battle, providing communications for forces in the area. With the German onslaught, the towns of Berdorf, Lauterborn, and Echternach were abandoned and a new front established to the west of Sauer along a line from Waldbillig, Consdorf, Osweiler, and Dickweiler.

On 19 December, Company A was ambushed and Tanks #13, #14, and #15 were hit. The crew of Tank #13 was captured and the crew of Tank #14 made its way back to friendly lines on foot. Two tanks, one from Company A and one from Company B, held off the enemy near Osweiler, and despite constant artillery fire, they continued to disrupt enemy attempts to take the town. Three tanks of Company B performed the same task at Dickweiler. On 21 December, the 70th was transferred from the U.S. First Army to the U.S. Third Army along with the 4th Division. The 70th and the 4th were badly in need of replacements and materiel because of the battle in the Hürtgen Forest. The following prayer was recited by General Patton on December 22, 1944:

> HEADQUARTERS
> THIRD UNITED STATES ARMY
> APO 403 U.S. ARMY
> 22 December 1944
>
> PRAYER
>
> Almighty and most merciful Father, we humbly beseech Thee, of Thy great goodness, to restrain these immoderate rains with which we have had to contend. Grant us fair weather for Battle. Graciously hearken to us as soldiers who call upon Thee that, armed with Thy power, we may advance from victory to victory, and crush the oppression and wickedness of our enemies, and establish Thy justice among men and nations.
>
> GEN. GEORGE PATTON

Snow continued to fall on 22 December, but later in the day the weather began to clear, allowing Allied air power to resume attacks on enemy formations. An attack on Osweiler with over a hundred enemy soldiers was repelled. The German Ardennes offensive under the command of Von Rundstedt was slowing, with advances grinding to a halt along the line that formed a large bulge. The Germans were overextended and Allied forces began to close off the escape route. The 70th engaged the enemy and repelled counterattacks from 23 to 24 December, with the loss of six tanks, one half-track, and one jeep. The German plan was to take Osweiler and Dickweiler on the first day of the attack so that panzer units could travel south and attack the city of Luxembourg. The actions by the 70th and 4th Division prevented this from happening. By 28 December, the battalion had moved into the city of Luxembourg for refitting and rehabilitation. Passes were given to visit the city, and the locals were friendly and grateful despite the occasional flights of enemy aircraft over the city. Toward the end of December, artillery barrages caused casualties to civilians there but had little effect on the 70th bivouac outside the city. The battalion continued refitting and rehabilitating, but was always on alert to move up at a moment's notice. January 1945 opened with light snow and cold weather. The Assault Gun Platoon returned on 3 January after being in fighting position near Herborn for over three weeks.

M4A3 76mm medium tank in winter camouflage, December 1944. DIXON

Looking up at an M4 in winter camouflage, winter 1944–45. DIXON

Captain Taynton next to a knocked-out Sturmgeschütz III, Germany, fall 1944. TAYNTON

German Wirbelwind self-propelled antiaircraft mount in winter camouflage, December 1944. The chassis is a Panzer IV. The four 2cm antiaircraft cannons have been removed along with other salvageable items. ERICKSON

This appears to be a medical-unit bus on the side of the road, December 1944. ERICKSON

M4 75mm medium tank knocked out on the side of the road, December 1944. ERICKSON

Panzer V Ausf. G knocked out on the side of the road, December 1944. ERICKSON

M4A3 76mm medium tank, probably disabled by a mine that damaged the track, December 1944. ERICKSON

Medium tank rolling through a German town, December 1944. ERICKSON

Loading ammunition in Hürtgenwald, December 1944. ERICKSON

M4A3 76mm medium tank in winter camouflage, December 1944. DIXON

M26A1 tank transporter hauling an M4 medium tank, winter 1944–45. DIXON

M4A3E8 (Easy 8). DIXON

M4A3 medium tank with 76mm gun, winter 1944–45. DIXON

M4A3 76mm medium tank in winter (whitewash) camouflage, December 1944. DIXON

M4A3 76mm medium tank carrying crew outside the armor, suggesting that they are not expecting immediate combat, December 1944. DIXON

M4 75mm welded-hull medium tank with M34A1 mantlet, December 1944. DIXON

Medium tanks in convoy. MCATEE

Company commander with M4A3 76mm medium tank in background, December 1944. DIXON

M4A3 76mm medium tank in winter camouflage with company commander in foreground. December 1944. DIXON

Captured Nazi flag, late 1944. Frank Anderson is on the right and John Dixon is second from the left. DIXON

M4 medium tank with three-piece transmission housing and M34A1 mantlet. KLEINHUIZEN

Clarence Kleinhuizen, December 1944. KLEINHUIZEN

Company B in Luxembourg City, January 1945. First row (left to right): Clarence Kleinhuizen, Clarence Jay, Edgar Morrison, Clarence McNamee. Back row (left to right): Eugene Mayberry, Howard Ellsworth, Alpha England. KLEINHUIZEN

View of D Company tank driving through medium-tank column, spring 1945. ERICKSON

M4 medium tank undergoing track maintenance, Germany, 1945. TAYNTON

Supply unit of the 70th Tank Battalion. From left to right: Charles J. Schwartz, Richard F. McCoy, and Anthony E. Schwoyer, Germany, 1945. TAYNTON

On 16 January 1945, the 70th relocated to another bivouac area at Reuland, Luxembourg. Companies B and D moved to the town of Godbrange, Luxembourg; the battalion command post moved to Café Würth; Company A, 1st Platoon, moved to Keuvelbach, and 2nd Platoon to Ermsdorf, Luxembourg; and Company B, 1st Platoon, moved to Medernach, Luxembourg. On 18 January, Company A, 2nd Platoon, moved in the vicinity of Ermsdorf to support the 1st Battalion, 8th Infantry, which had established a bridgehead across the Sauer River northeast of Bettendorf. Due to icy road conditions, the vehicles had difficulty traveling on roads. The medium and light tanks easily slid sideways off the road, causing delay.

On 19 January, 70th tanks attached to the 8th Infantry Regiment crossed the Sauer River near Gilsdorf. By the end of the day, all vehicles had crossed, and Companies A and B cleaned out several machine-gun nests that hampered infantry advance. The attack continued the next day, reducing the extent of the bulge formed in December. On 21 January, two tanks from Company B moved on Tandel, Luxembourg, and knocked out an enemy tank. On 22 January, Company B engaged enemy tanks at Fouhren and met stiff resistance. Reinforcements arrived the next day and helped break up the enemy counterattack, overrunning two enemy tanks, an 88mm antitank gun, and two 75mm antitank guns.

Company B, 1st Platoon attacked Klein Reisdorf. Company D attacked in the vicinity of Bettendorf, Luxembourg, with the 8th Infantry. Weather conditions and materiel shortages plagued the 70th during this advance.

All companies received new replacements on 26 January, and on the twenty-seventh, the 70th was transferred back to VIII Corps after an attachment to XII Corps. On the twenty-eighth, the 70th moved through Larochette, Mersch, Attert, Bastogne, and Basbellain with the 3rd Platoon of Company B in Elcherath, Germany. The next day, 1st and 3rd Platoons of Company B supported the 2nd Battalion, 12th Infantry Regiment, in an attack at Bleialf. When climbing a steep hill on the way to an attack from Ihren to Grosslangenfeld, all tanks of 3rd Platoon were chained together. The lead tank was hit, stalling the advance, and the unit had to withdraw. Muddy conditions, numerous mines, and accurate antitank fire also stalled the advance, contributing to the retreat. On 5 February, 1st Platoon, Company A, moved with 2nd Battalion, 12th Infantry Regiment, in support of an attack south and east of Schlausenbadl.

INTO GERMANY

As the platoon moved through the woods, it received fire from a German self-propelled gun, which hit two tanks. Company A attacked the position, and the enemy surrendered. Company B then supported Company C in an attack on the town of Brandscheid. Company C attacked through the town and onto the Siegfried Line northeast of Brandscheid. The 70th tanks supplied covering fire, while the infantry snuck up to pillboxes and placed satchel charges. Enemy troops infiltrated back into the town of Brandscheid, occupying several fortifications and pillboxes, and counterattacked the next day. Company C, 1st Platoon, moved to quell the attack, and severe fighting ensued, but the attack was neutralized by noon as the 1st Platoon cleaned out the remnants. The 3rd Platoon, Company C, held off the enemy at the northwest part of town from repeated attacks. On 6 February, 3rd Platoon, Company C, attacked Niedermehlen, encountering stiff resistance from infantry fortifications and self-propelled guns. The opposing force, 2nd SS Division, counterattacked, causing the 70th to withdraw with the lead tank of the 3rd Platoon destroyed by antitank guns. Headquarters Battalion moved to Buchet while two tanks from Company A supported an attack at Gondenbrett, but were driven back by heavy enemy artillery and rocket fire to a position near Wascheid. The 2nd and 3rd Platoons of Company D (light tanks) repulsed a counterattack outside the city of Prüm, taking approximately eighty prisoners.

Back row (left to right): Albert Lennex, unknown, Eugene Mayberry, Tom Young, unknown, Edgar Morrison, Alpha England, unknown, Clarence McNamee, unknown, Warren Renschler. Front row (left to right): Ralph Yeatts (platoon sergeant), Irving Frank, unknown behind Kleinhuizen and to right of Yeatts, Clarence Kleinhuizen, Elio Papucci, Mike Jones, James Webster (driver), Clarence Jay, Edward Gossler, and Willis Mills. February 1945. KNOEBEL

Dozer tank pushing dirt and debris into a large hole to repair a bridge. TAYNTON

Disabled Panzer V "Panther" Ausf. G, spring 1945. DECARLO

A column of the 70th crossing a creek in early 1945. This appears to be a Company D column, as evidenced by the light tank. ERICKSON

Typical German machine-gun bunker. The 70th used flamethrower tanks to successfully defeat these emplacements. ERICKSON

Jagdpanzer 38 tank destroyer knocked out in Germany, early 1945. ERICKSON

M3 half-track of Headquarters Company, spring 1945. Note the Joe Peckerwood on the armor behind the driver's seat. ERICKSON

Lieutenant Colonel Davidson, now commander of the 70th, surveying the terrain for the next operation, spring 1945. ERICKSON

M4A3E8 76mm medium tank with Private McAtee in the photograph, January 1945. This was one of the few tanks with a muzzle brake on the main gun, which made the vehicle look like a German tank. Many tankers worried about being mistaken for the enemy. MCATEE

Messerschmitt 262 jet fighter, April 1945, located near what appears to be an Autobahn, which these aircraft would use as runways. This was the first operational jet fighter of World War II. This aircraft appeared toward the end of the war and was often hidden in a forest. MCATEE

German Junkers 52 tri-motor. Used by many airlines in Europe prior to the war, they became a primary German transport aircraft during the war. MCATEE

Private McAtee in front of his M4A1 cast-hull medium tank. MCATEE

M4A3E2 Jumbo 76mm assault tank of the 70th with Mike DeCarlo in the driver's hatch. This tank had thicker armor than the standard medium tank. Note the Sommerfeld netting for inserting tree branches for camouflage. This is a rare photo, since only 254 of these tanks were made. The 70th received these tanks after November 1944, but this picture appears to have been taken in the spring of 1945. DECARLO

Clarence Kleinhuizen displaying a captured Nazi flag, spring 1945. KLEINHUIZEN

M4A1 76mm medium tank for Company A, 2nd Platoon, 70th Tank Battalion, spring 1945. DIXON

Relaxing in camp. LARSON

Lt. Roger McKitrick standing in front of a German Messerschmitt Bf 110 fighter aircraft, Germany, 1945. LARSON

M4A3E8 medium tank with 76mm gun and welded hull, Kitzingen, Germany, April 1945. This model tank was often called the "Easy 8." Lieutenant McKitrick is sitting on the tank. LARSON

Destroyed railroad tracks, possibly damaged deliberately by the Germans as they retreated. ERICKSON

Typical 70th camp with an M29 Weasel cargo carrier shown to the left. ERICKSON

Ludendorff Bridge at Remagen, March 1945. CONNORS

The Ludendorff Bridge was found intact as the Allied armies approached. Efforts by the Germans to destroy the bridge were unsuccessful, and several Allied units crossed it. On 17 March 1945, the bridge collapsed despite attempts to reinforce it. U.S. ARMY

Crew of an M3 half-track adjusting tracks before moving out. Note the S-1 and S-4 signs on the left rear of the vehicle, suggesting that this was a Headquarters Company vehicle. TAYNTON

Gambsheim train station, March 1945. DECARLO

Company A, 3rd Platoon, moved up to support Company D to repulse any additional assaults by the enemy from the town of Prüm, which was located in a valley with narrow, easily defended roads entering the town. Several enemy trenches, mortar, and artillery positions just outside the town were shelled by Allied artillery. As usual, the battalion was split up with Company A, 2nd Platoon, attacking Gondenbrett to clear out enemy positions, Company B, 3rd Platoon, clearing the town of Steinplehien, and 2nd and 3rd Platoons of Company C attacking Neidermehien. In this attack, three enemy tanks were knocked out and approximately 200 prisoners taken as the company moved to defensive positions outside the town to repel a counterattack.

On 10 February 1945, 1st Platoon, Company A, supported an attack by Company E of the 2nd Battalion (22nd Infantry Regiment) on the town of Hermespand. The enemy put up a fierce counterattack, and artillery had to be called in to quell it. A squad of infantry supporting each tank fought through the town, clearing out enemy positions. Approximately forty enemy dead were found and fifty taken prisoner. Snipers became a problem, but were cleared out quickly as the 70th and infantry set up defensive positions.

Company B, 3rd Platoon, cleared out remaining resistance in the town of Steinmehien using high-explosive rounds on buildings where enemy soldiers were hidden in cellars. The collapse of buildings hit by high-explosive fire forced whoever was hiding in the cellar to immediately leave the premises.

Company C's 1st and 3rd Platoons, with infantry support, attacked enemy soldiers in houses southeast of Prüm, causing the enemy to withdraw despite an attack by a German tank, which knocked out Tank #2 of 1st Platoon but was later destroyed by other tanks. The roads were cleared of mines and the tanks made ready for an assault through Prüm and Hermespand.

On 1 March, a big push was organized. Company A, minus 1st Platoon, was attached to Combat Team 8 with 1st Platoon in reserve. Company B remained at Battalion HQ, while Company C in Dausfeld was attached to Combat Team 22 and Company D was attached to Combat Team 8. The Assault Gun Platoon was attached to 290th Field Artillery Battalion. The next few days saw engagement with enemy forces at various small towns near Prüm: Weinsheim, Dausfeld, Willwerath, Niesen, Baselt, and Gondelsheim. On 3 March, 1st Platoon of Company A was attached to 3rd Battalion, 22nd Combat Team, to clear the town of Weinsheim. The 2nd and 3rd Platoons of Company A advanced toward Gondelsheim, clearing the road as they advanced on the town. Just outside town, Tanks #6, #7, #10, and #13 were hit by antitank fire, halting the advance, and resulting in a withdrawal to assess positions of antitank fire. At the same time, Company B attacked and captured the town of Rommersheim, inflicting many enemy casualties and taking many prisoners despite the loss of Tank #13. Company C attacked and occupied the town of Weinsheim. The attack on the town of Gondelsheim, with Company D supporting Company A, was stalled with intense antitank fire, with three tanks from Company A and three tanks from Company D knocked out. On 3 March, Prüm fell to the advance, and on 4 March the battalion command post was moved into Prüm, which had been badly damaged as a result of the fighting, with few buildings standing. The streets in the town were impassable and had to be cleared by dozers.

On 4 March, 1st and 3rd Platoons of Company A attacked Gondelsheim again with attached tank destroyers, and Company D took the town. Company B supported an attack on the towns of Budesheim, Fleringen, and Wallersheim, taking enemy positions and clearing out opposition. Company C engaged in fighting near Weinsheim, north of Gondelsheim, with Tank #1 knocked out from mines, causing the unit to move back to Prüm. The 3rd Platoon bivouacked at Schwirzheim for the night. On 5 March, having defeated several enemy strong points, 1st Platoon, Company B, moved to support an attack on the town of Oos, which was captured that day. The 2nd and 3rd Platoons of Company B moved through Budesheim unopposed. The 1st and 3rd Platoons of Company C supported the 22nd Combat Team in an attack on Duppach, firing on enemy targets despite artillery from German units. On 6 March, 1st Platoon, Company B, moved from the town of Oos to attack Mullendorf under heavy enemy artillery, small-arms, and machine-gun fire. Although no antitank fire was encountered, tank commanders were typically vulnerable as they often had to look out of the turret hatch to determine what was going on.

The Allies occupied Mullendorf in the afternoon and the unit moved on toward the town of Roth, which they took after a fierce battle with enemy forces in the woods as they approached the town. On 7 March, all units of the 70th reverted to battalion control (less Company C, which was attached to the 22nd Combat Team) in preparation for Task Force Rhino under command of Gen. James S. Rodwell, including 8th Infantry Division (mechanized), 29th Field Artillery Battalion–Company A, 4th Medical Battalion–Company A, 4th Engineer Combat Battalion, 4th Reconnaissance Troop (mechanized), 377th AAA Battalion–Battery C, 4th Signal Company, and 610th Tank Destroyer Battalion–Company A attached to the 70th. The mission was to advance as rapidly as possible to the high ground near the town of Reifferscheid. Lieutenant Colonel Davidson of the 70th was in command of the assault force. On 9 March, the Task Force Rhino assault force moved to the objective in the following order: 4th Reconnaissance Troop, 1st Platoon Company D–70th, Company B–70th, a platoon of tank destroyers, 70th HQ tanks, Company A–70th, another platoon of tank destroyers, 70th Battalion Staff Section, 2nd Platoon Company D–70th, and the 3rd Platoon of the tank destroyers. The remainder of the force followed under the command of Col. Richard G. McKee. Having crossed the Kyll, the task force found little resistance until reaching the town of Kerpen, where the lead tanks encountered a German platoon that sustained casualties and was captured.

The task force then moved to Üxheim, where one enemy tank was destroyed. (At this stage in the war, the Germans were unable to muster large formations of tanks.) At this point, one of the M5 light tanks was hit by an antitank gun. The Assault Gun Platoon immediately fired upon and destroyed the position. The assault force rapidly progressed to the town of Adenau on the morning of 9 March and, despite road obstacles, moved through the town with Company B leading with infantry support. The assault was so rapid that the bridges in the town were not destroyed, and German troops awakened to the presence of the American assault force. The enemy abandoned their equipment, leaving their positions in a state of disarray with documents, communications equipment, and other command-related materials strewn about. There was a feeling among the task force that enemy morale was low, as the opposition was becoming less intense.

Word came down that most of the German forces were east of the Rhine; the 9th Infantry Division had crossed at Remagen, and the Third Army was consolidating on the west bank of the river. All forces were moving rapidly to take advantage of the enemy retreat. With the completion of Task Force Rhino's mission, the 70th, less Company C, bivouacked in the town of Adenau. Then on 10 March, they moved in the vicinity of Auel, where they refitted and repaired vehicles. During the 24 hours of Operation Task Force Rhino, the 70th advanced 18 miles and captured 1,541 enemy soldiers and a large amount of equipment, including American equipment the Germans had captured during the Ardennes offensive. It was common for the Germans to utilize Russian, French, and American equipment in their arsenal of weapons.

On 10 March, the 70th was transferred to the 6th Army Group and attached to the Seventh Army. Vehicle maintenance and refitting occurred on 11 March, and on 12 March the entire battalion moved to Merch and set up camp for the night. The move required traveling over a distance of 72 miles on hard surface roads, taking a toll on vehicle tracks. The battalion was attached to XXI Corps, 63rd Infantry Division (which was newly formed). Company A was attached to the 254th Infantry Regiment, and Company B to the 255th Infantry Regiment. On 15 March, Company A launched an attack, supported by the 254th, against Ensheim, which was captured that day. Meanwhile, Company B, with the support of the 255th, captured Ormesheim. Several of these attacks occurred at night, so the tanks used dimly cast searchlights so the Allied infantry could recognize them as Allied vehicles. Company C moved to a staging area under enemy artillery fire near Kleinblittersdorf.

On 16 March, Company A attacked pillboxes and other fortifications near Ensheim. Over 240 artillery rounds were fired at the Siegfried Line to allow infantry to advance, while the Assault Gun Platoon shelled the city of Saarbrucken. On 17 March, Companies A and B progressed rapidly. The next day, the 70th was relieved by the 740th Tank Battalion, attached to the 4th Infantry Division, and moved to a bivouac 2,000 yards north of the city of Sarreguemines for refitting, maintenance, and preparation for the next operation. Allied forces were advancing rapidly, and on 20 March, the 70th had to move 80 miles to contact the enemy at Hochfelden.

Captain Taynton in Germany, spring 1945. TAYNTON

On 28 March, after driving 104 miles, the battalion arrived at Wachenheim, and began crossing the Rhine at the city of Worms on 29 March. The unit crossed on pontoon bridges in about two hours along with the 12th Armored Division. With infantry mounted on tanks because of the rapid movement, the 70th plowed through makeshift roadblocks such as trees, logs, and old vehicles under light rear-guard fire, suggesting that the ability of the enemy to resist was dwindling. Schneeburg, Hardheim, Tauberbischofsheim, Königheim, Dillieheim, and Mudau were captured along with bridges over the Tauber River.

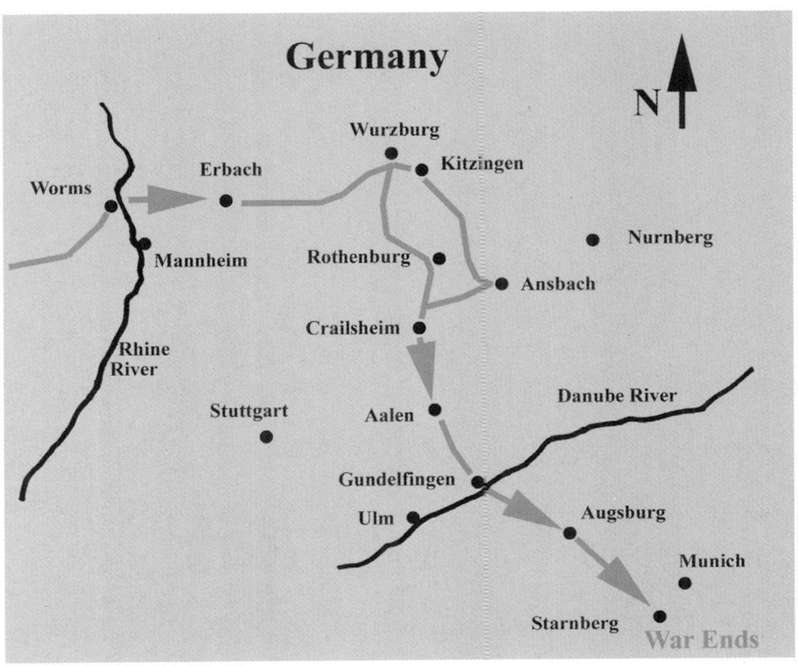

The 70th's route through Germany. ROBERTS

Mike DeCarlo, tank driver, in front of his M4, Germany, 1945. Note the duckbill track used to enhance performance on soft ground. These were easily broken off in uneven terrain. DECARLO

Mike DeCarlo in Saarbrucken, Germany, 20 March 1945. DECARLO

Tank platoon. DECARLO

Knocked-out medium tank, early 1945. DECARLO

Overhauling a tank engine. From left to right: Joseph P. Tilley, Gray, Wahl, and Fissell. Germany, 1945. ISAACS

Early April found the 70th advancing rapidly from town to town with little resistance. On 14 April, the front shifted to the southwest toward the Alps with light enemy resistance. A typical situation for the 70th as they rolled through a town would include enemy small-arms fire, their return fire, and the enemy retreat to the woods and later surrender. Enemy prisoners marched to the rear in an orderly fashion and would be picked up by military police, suggesting that these troops were happy to be finished with the war.

The town of Steinach was defended by the German 1st Mountain Regiment, and after the initial attack and later counterattack, the mountain troops were pushed out of the town. The towns of Richelshofen and Fliwingshofen were lightly defended, but many towns did not put up a fight. On 15 April, 1st and 2nd Platoons of Company C ran into stiff opposition in taking of the town of Blumweiler, which was defended by many roadblocks and mines. On 16 April, 1st Platoon, Company A, encountered stiff resistance while capturing Bergel before moving on to Oberdachstetten. Company B attacked and cleared the towns of Schwensdorf and Nordenberg. Company C attacked and occupied the town of Leuzendorf. On 17 April, Company A was attached to a task force to capture the town of Ansbach.

Tank retrievers in Germany, 1945. CONNORS

From left to right: Capt. Gordon R. Brodie, Col. Henry E. Davidson Jr., Capt. James D. McLanachan, and Maj. Kenneth J. Krach in Kitzingen, Germany, 1945. BRODIE

A 70th Tank Battalion column moving out for action against the enemy, approximately March 1945. The first tank is an M4A3 76mm gun, early turret. The second tank is an M4A3E8 with 76mm gun. The third tank is an M4A1 75mm gun with M34 gun mount. The fourth tank is an M4 with three-piece differential housing and M34 gun mount. A dozer tank can be seen in the background. The truck on the hill is a CCKW 353 deuce and a half. ERICKSON

The town of Colmberg was heavily defended, and the tanks were deployed to take the town. The task force continued across country and took the town of Hinteholz. A supply train drawn by horses was destroyed. It was obvious at this time during the war that the Germans probably could not hold out much longer since their supplies were being hauled by animals and humans using carts rather than motorized transport. The towns of Hoffen and Ansbach were taken by midnight. Company B approached Rothenberg and encountered light resistance until they reached the town, where antitank fire halted the advance. Company C captured Lohrbach and Buch with light enemy resistance.

On 20 April 1945, two platoons of Company C attacked Crailsheim, capturing the town that day. Task Force Rodwell was formed on 21 April at the town of Völkershausen, with all units of the 70th participating. Company B of the 610 Tank Destroyer Battalion and one platoon from Company B of the 4th Engineer Battalion were attached to the 70th, with Lieutenant Colonel Davidson in command of the assault group and Maj. Kenneth J. Krach in command of the assault infantry. The infantry was motorized, and a platoon of light tanks guarded the rear echelon. The task force advanced through Horschausen, Ellrichshausen, and Crailsheim. Crailsheim was difficult in that the task force encountered enemy artillery rounds as well as roadblocks. Soft ground from recent rains caused many vehicles to get stuck, and these had to be towed to solid ground. That evening, the task force reached the town of Jagstzell, where the enemy had destroyed the bridge, halting the advance until the next morning when the bridge and road were made passable.

National Socialist flag and Women's Guild National Socialist banner captured by Corporal McAtee in late April 1945. The town name, Jagstzell, was sewn on the banners. ROBERTS

The task force moved on through Hutten toward Leinenfirst, which was heavily defended by an SS company. A short fight ensued with the enemy escaping to the south, although the task force took many prisoners. The assault guns fired eighty high-explosive rounds into the town of Neuler, which was defended by an SS unit, and the tanks moved in under heavy small-arms fire. The infantry dismounted and fought with the enemy in close urban combat. The lead tank was hit by Panzerfaust fire and enemy troops jumped onto the tank to kill the crew. A neighboring tank fired its machine gun, driving the enemy off the tank. The town was cleared in about two hours, with many enemy prisoners taken. The task force moved toward Sulzdorf onto high ground overlooking the valley toward the objective, the town of Aalen. With the help of German civilians, a roadblock was cleared at the town of Wasseralfingen. Many German civilians were tired of the war and cooperated with the Allies. They hated the SS troops who often brutalized fellow countrymen. German civilians had warned that over a thousand SS troops defended the town of Aalen. The next day the Assault Gun Platoon fired on roads leading out of the town to the south to prevent enemy movement.

Wittighausen train station just northeast of Nuremburg, April 1945. ERICKSON

M4A3 76mm medium tanks stuck on the side of a narrow road, southern Germany, 1945. ISAACS

On 23 April, Company A moved on Aalen with the 1st Battalion, 12th Combat Team, along with Company C and the 3rd Battalion. The attack met little resistance until the center of town, where antitank and self-propelled guns were set up in defensive positions. Tank #6 was knocked out. As the fight developed, with Company C moving in from the north, the enemy decided to retreat to the south, but was caught by Company B. Realizing it was hopeless, many men surrendered with their equipment.

On 24 April, Task Force Rodell moved southeast toward Gundelfingen, led by Company C with the 2nd Battalion, 12th Infantry Regiment. Local civilians warned of three enemy tanks that had passed by earlier and helped clear a minefield near the town of Unt-Kochen. The attack continued through Ebnat and on to Mattheim where many enemy troops were captured. The next towns were Oggenhausen, Giengen, Hermarigen, and Brenz, where the inhabitants waved flags welcoming the Allied force as it passed through. The task force met up with the 12th Armored Division and became inactive as the attached units were reassigned. On 25 April, Company A moved across the Danube River at Lauingen. The next day, Company A advanced along the Autobahn toward Wollbach and Kutzenhausen. Company B attacked through several towns and spent the night in Wengen. On 27 April, Company A advanced through several towns and by dark bivouacked at Lechfeld Airport, while Company B moved on to the town of Willishausen.

Allied forces rapidly advanced through the Brenner Pass, and the enemy retreated, knowing that the war would probably be over shortly. On 30 April, the 70th reached Starnberg, with some elements heading farther south. The 70th set up camps in Starnberg (Headquarters and Service Companies), Gauting (Company A), Eglsee (B Company), Hohen Schäftlarn (Company C), and Wolfrathshausen (Company D). On 2 May, the battalion was transferred from the Seventh to the Third Army, which was still attacking into Czechoslovakia. On 7 May, the 70th started to move out to the next attack when suddenly, and unofficially, word came down that the war was over. As with most units, they were ordered to hold fast in defensive mode until the official surrender occurred on 8 May 1945, in the event that some enemy units had not received orders to stand down. Word came from SHAEF at 1400 hours while the 70th was on its way to Ingolstadt, after leaving Munich that morning.

The 70th continued on to a location near Starnberg. Headquarters Company camped at Sandersdorf; Service Company at Wackerstein; Company B at Steinsdorf; Company C at Gross Mehring; Company A near Ingolstadt; and D Company at an old castle on the cliff overlooking the Danube at Dünzing. The route of march was Starnberg, Gauting, Munich to Ingolstadt.

All elements of the 70th spent the next few days servicing equipment and setting up camp. All company commanders inspected the area, noting the location of enemy equipment, factories, prison camps, roads, bridges, and other points. On 15 May, Service and B Companies moved to Rothenberg. On 17 May, all elements of the 70th moved to Rothenberg with the exception of Company D, which moved to Sandersdorf to patrol the area and set up prison camps and checkpoints. Company D later rejoined the battalion.

Civilians gathering in front of what appears to be a camp.
ERICKSON

A 70th tank driving along the road near a camp.
ERICKSON

Robert Knoebel (gunner) on the left, Edward Jones (tank commander) center front, Charles Miller (bow gunner) on the right, and Warren Renschler (loader) on top, Company B, Bavaria, 1945. KNOEBEL

Nurses of the 131st Evacuation Hospital on a Headquarters Company M4 medium tank of the 70th Tank Battalion, Germany, 1945: Margaret Catter (in turret), Mary Maguire (in assistant driver's hatch), and Ann Doyle (on the main gun). ROBERTS

Nurse Mary Maguire of the 131st Evacuation Hospital on a 70th Headquarters Company medium tank, Germany, 1945. ROBERTS

CHAPTER 8

The End of the War

ROTHENBERG, BAMBERG

The 70th settled down to postwar status in Rothenberg on the Tauber River. Patrols were sent out to round up enemy holdouts with the help of the local civilians. Saboteurs were suspected of damaging communication lines, but over time these incidents decreased. The local population reported on suspicious personnel since they were eager to get back to a peacetime way of life. Captain Brodie was placed in command of a POW camp, which initially received approximately two hundred prisoners. On 21 May, Company D arrived from Sandersdorf and moved into quarters in the "Realschule" with Service Company. There were movies and lectures on redeployment to the Far East and the expected invasion of Japan. However, by mid-August, the war in the Far East was over and the 70th settled into an occupation status, guarding their sector and rounding up those still hostile to the occupiers. A point system was developed whereby a large number of points was awarded to personnel with long overseas service time, allowing them to return home before others who had fewer points. Many of the 70th personnel who had survived since North Africa had accumulated enough points to go home.

Headquarters of the 70th in Rothenberg, May 1945. TAYNTON

Company D on parade in Rothenburg, 1945. TAYNTON

Sign for 70th Headquarters. TAYNTON

Captain Connors on the morning after a celebration in his honor before his departure for the States, June 1945. He had spent forty-two months in North Africa and Europe. CONNORS

18 May/45	Camp Tilley	Rothenberg, Germany
11 June/45	Contentment Camp	Bamberg, Germany

Camps of the 70th in Germany after the war. TAYNTON

German prisoners helping Service Company repair a jeep, summer 1945. ISAACS

American units consolidating after the German surrender. ERICKSON

Headquarters Company in an intact home. TAYNTON

Clarence Kleinhuizen on leave in Rothenburg, Germany, summer 1945. KLEINHUIZEN

Clarence Kleinhuizen at the pool in Rothenburg, Germany, summer 1945. KLEINHUIZEN

Warrant Officer Arrington B. Turner. TURNER

City Hall, Rothenburg, on the Tauber.
TAYNTON

Three photos taken by Captain Taynton of the devastation in Germany after the war. TAYNTON

French 27.4cm K(E) 592 (f) railway gun "Cäsar" being inspected by 70th personnel on leave, summer 1945. ERICKSON

Downtown Rothenburg, summer 1945. TAYNTON

Looking along the gun barrel of the rail gun "Cäsar," summer 1945. ERICKSON

Wrecked Sd.Kfz. 179 Bergepanther in Germany, 1945. TAYNTON

Captain Taynton in the front of a Panzer V Ausf. A "Panther" in Germany. TAYNTON

A Panzer III in a training area in Germany. TAYNTON

Frontal view of the same aircraft shown below. ERICKSON

Mistel piggyback aircraft photo taken by Sergeant Erickson in Gardelegen, Germany, in the summer of 1945. The bottom aircraft is a Junkers 88 while the top aircraft is an FW 190. After the pair took off, the FW 190 guided the Junkers, which was filled with explosives, toward the target and then released it. ERICKSON

Junkers 88 nightfighter. ERICKSON

Replacements were received as veteran 70th soldiers rotated home on the point system, leaving the personnel in the battalion almost unrecognizable compared to its composition in 1942. On 27 May, a formation was held in the Sportplaz, awarding Bronze Stars and Purple Hearts to 70th personnel.

On 9 June 1945 the battalion received orders to move stateside, and they traveled to a marshaling area near Podeldorf with the 4th Division. The route to the transport area from Rothenburg was through Windsheim, Neustadt, Hockstadt, and Bamberg. The 70th was detached from the 4th Division, having worked with them since 11 March 1944. Gen. Harold W. Blakeley of the 4th signed the detachment order with regret, since the 70th and 4th had a very close working relationship.

Major Taynton preparing to take the battalion back to the States. KNOEBEL

Sign photographed by Major Taynton upon entering Austria, summer 1945. TAYNTON

Major Taynton on leave in Brenner, Austria, summer 1945. TAYNTON

Outskirts of Berlin, 1945. CONNORS

The Brenner Pass is the main route between Austria and Italy and was used extensively by the Germans during the war. It was also an escape route for Nazis attempting to leave Germany after the end of the war. TAYNTON

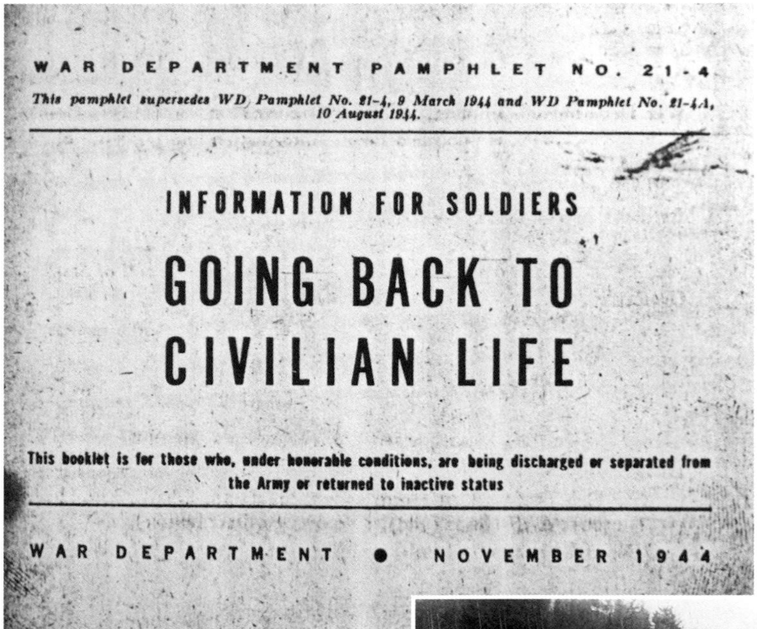

WAR DEPARTMENT PAMPHLET NO. 21-4

This pamphlet supersedes WD Pamphlet No. 21-4, 9 March 1944 and WD Pamphlet No. 21-4A, 10 August 1944.

INFORMATION FOR SOLDIERS

GOING BACK TO CIVILIAN LIFE

This booklet is for those who, under honorable conditions, are being discharged or separated from the Army or returned to inactive status

WAR DEPARTMENT ● NOVEMBER 1944

An instruction manual for those looking forward to returning home. ROBERTS

Empty German Autobahn, summer 1945.
TAYNTON

European "Forty and Eight" boxcars used to haul passengers immediately after the war, summer 1945. Most of the passenger cars had been destroyed by this point. The nickname "Forty and Eight" originated in World War I when Americans were told that each boxcar could carry forty soldiers or eight horses.
TAYNTON

Lieutenant Colonel Davidson conversing with staff members and a major general, summer 1945. TAYNTON

Tanks from the 70th parked on a street with several children looking on, summer 1945. The first vehicle is an M4A3 76mm, the second is an M4A1 76mm, and the third is an M4A3E8. It was common for the 70th to have a variety of models of medium tanks. Most of these vehicles were given to foreign governments and never returned to the States. TAYNTON

M26 Pershing heavy tank that was issued late in the war and was used by some armored divisions, summer 1945. The 70th was not issued this tank during the war, although many tankers wished they had the 90mm gun to battle the Germans. TAYNTON

During this time, the 70th received the new M26 Pershing tanks with 90mm guns, which could attack German tanks successfully in a frontal assault. The 70th tankers were impressed with the new tanks as they trained with them to prepare for further combat in the Far East. They never got a chance to use them in that theater, as the Japanese surrendered in August 1945. After a month of training, the 70th moved to Panzer Kaserne in Bamberg on 6 July 1945. The 70th settled into a noncombat environment with a tank parking area, an officers' club, an enlisted men's club, a maintenance building, and indoor kitchen facilities. Passes were available to the Riviera, Switzerland, Brussels, the Alps, and Berchtesgaden.

Zeke Penez, crewman with Francis Ross, Nuremberg, 1945. ROSS

Company D parked at Panzer Kaserne in Bamberg. ROSS

Medium tank M4A3E8 76mm with .50-caliber gunner at the firing range in Germany, 1945. Gunnery practice continued after the German surrender in anticipation of being transferred to the Far East theater. TAYNTON

Medium tank M4A3 76mm at the firing range. TAYNTON

A new M24 light tank (Chaffee) at the firing range. This vehicle was intended to replace the M5 Stuart light tank. TAYNTON

A new M26 Pershing heavy tank at the firing range. TAYNTON

Crew from an M26 displaying a 90mm cartridge. TAYNTON

View of the "Eagle's Nest" at Berchtesgaden, Hitler's conference center overlooking the Bavarian Alps. He actually lived a few miles down the road at the Berghoff. The photo was taken in the summer of 1945 while Major Taynton was on leave. TAYNTON

The 70th moved to Nuremberg on 4 September 1945, with Companies C and D quartered in barracks just east of the stadium and the remainder quartered on the northern outskirts of the city. Guard posts were set up throughout the town during the Nuremberg war trials. As the 70th reorganized, the new battalion commander, Maj. Harry J. Kenny, realized that there were very few trained tankers in the 70th because the experienced personnel had rotated home. Consequently, a battalion-wide training course was instituted, teaching tactics and how to operate the new tanks, and practice firing at the old panzer range.

The course also involved demonstrations of new tanks traveling over obstacles and crashing through trees, which was a big hit with the new replacements. By April and May 1946, the 70th was deactivated and moved to Fort Knox, to be reactivated on 1 August 1946 as part of the armored school.

Tank D17 in Nuremberg, Germany, 1945. ROSS

Company D in Nuremberg, Germany, summer 1945. ROSS

Awards ceremony, summer 1945. TAYNTON

Offer of a handshake to a Russian soldier, summer 1945. TAYNTON

Russian sentry at his guardhouse, summer 1945. TAYNTON

Lt. Roger McKitrick presenting a portrait of Maj. Gen. W. G. Livesay. The writing on the photo says, "To Lt. Roger H. McKitrick. In appreciation of his good work. W. G. Livesay." LARSON

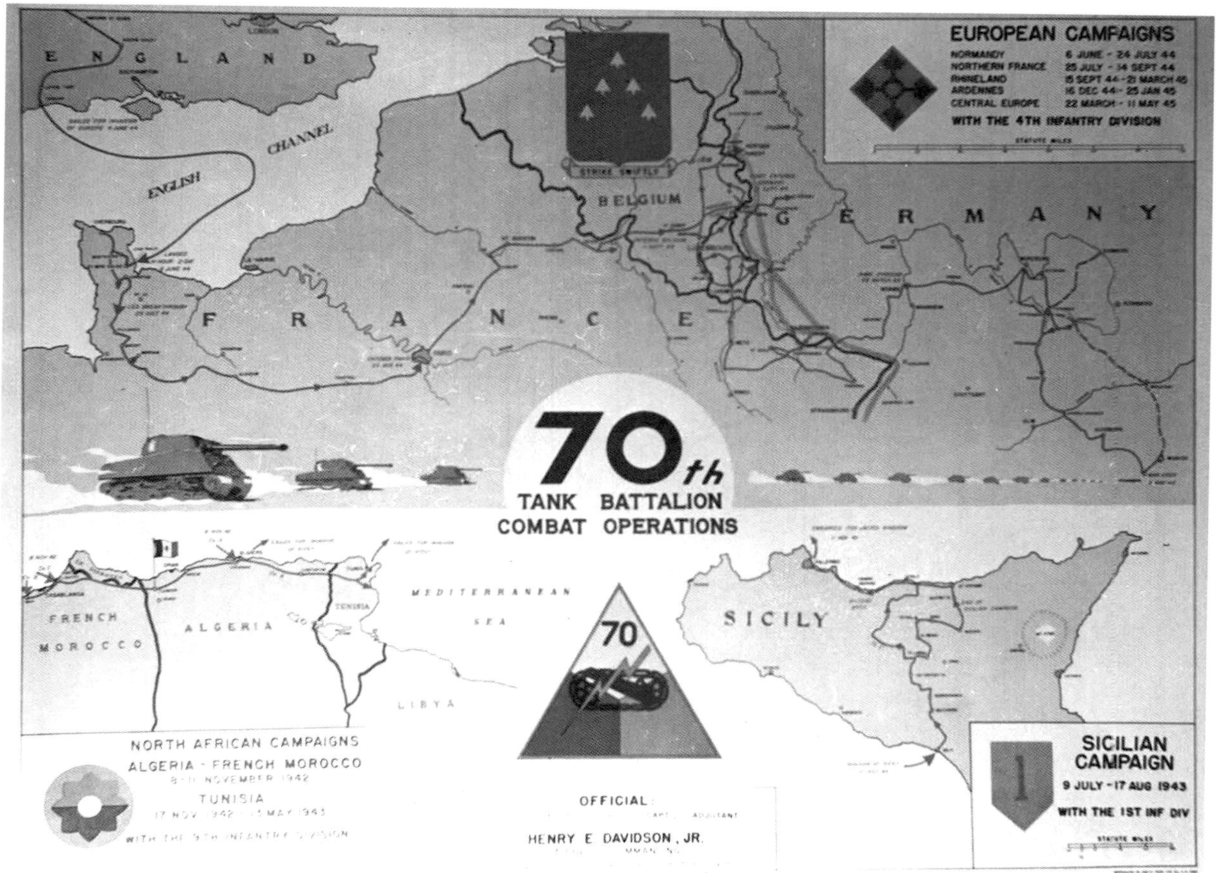

Drawing by Lieutenant McKitrick depicting the campaigns of the 70th, summer 1948. TAYNTON

Lieutenant McKitrick presenting his drawing of the campaigns to the 70th Battalion commander, summer 1948. TAYNTON

Cleaned-up jeep. TAYNTON

Members of the 70th Battalion getting ready to embark for the States, summer 1945. Those who had served the longest and had the highest number of points traveled to a holding camp like Camp Lucky Strike to await their ship assignment. TAYNTON

References

Anderson, Walter T. Individual Deceased Personnel File.

Bando, Mark. *101st Airborne, the Screaming Eagles at Normandy*. Osceola, WI: MBI Publishing, 2001.

Bando, Mark. *Breakout at Normandy: The 2nd Armored Division in the Land of the Dead*. Osceola, WI: MBI Publishing, 1999.

Brodie, Gordon. Diary. 70th Tank Battalion Company D. Roberts Armory Collection.

Burgett, Don, veteran of the 101st Airborne, World War II. Conversations with author, 2009–14.

Burgett, Donald R. *Currahee! A Screaming Eagle at Normandy*. New York: Bantam Dell Publishing, 1967.

Ciaravella, Frank, veteran of the 70th Tank Battalion, World War II. Conversations with author, 1999–2004

Claxon, Sean, historian, Normandy, World War II. Conversations with author, 2010; email correspondence, 2010–15

Company A. Diary. 70th Tank Battalion. Roberts Armory Collection

Company B. Diary. 70th Tank Battalion. Roberts Armory Collection

Company C. Diary. 70th Tank Battalion. Roberts Armory Collection

Company D. Diary. 70th Tank Battalion. Roberts Armory Collection

Crismon, Fred. *U.S. Military Wheeled Vehicles*. Sarasota, FL: Crestline, 1983.

Culver, Bruce. *Sherman in Action*. Carrollton, TX: Squadron/Signal, 1977.

Curry, Aaron D. Individual Deceased Personnel File.

Dail, Robert, North Africa and Sicily historian, World War II. Emails to author, 2011–15.

Drew, Richard, Atlantic Wall historian, World War II. Emails to author, 2011.

Fritz, John, veteran of the 70th Tank Battalion, World War II. Conversations with author, 1999–2003

Gawne, Jonathan. *Spearheading D-Day*. Paris: Histoire et Collections, 1998.

Goldstein, Donald, et al. *D-Day Normandy*. Herndon, VA: Brassey's, 1994.

Hall, Chester B. *History of the 70th Tank Battalion, 5 June, 1940 . . . 22 May, 1946*. Louisville, KY: Southern Press, 1946.

Henkemans, Niels, historian, specialist U.S. and German armor, Normandy, World War II. Emails to author, 2010–15.

Hunnicutt, R. P. *History of the American Light Tank*. Novato, CA: Presidio, 1992.

Isaacs, Buck, veteran of the 70th Tank Battalion, World War II. Conversations with author, 2008–15.

Jensen, Marvin. *Strike Swiftly: The 70th Tank Battalion; From North Africa to Normandy to Germany*. New York: Presidio Press, 1997.

Jensen, Marvin, veteran of the 70th Tank Battalion, World War II. Conversations with author, 1998–2001.

Jewell, Brian, and Mike Chappell. *British Battledress 1937–61*. London: Reed International, 1981.

Malatesta, John, veteran of the 70th Tank Battalion, World War II. Conversations with author, 2011–14.

Mesko, Jim. *M3 Half-tracks in Action*. Carrollton, TX: Squadron/Signal, 1996.

Messinger, Charles. *The D-Day Atlas*. New York: Thames and Hudson, 2004.

Ross, Eric. *Biography of Sgt. Francis Ross, Company D, 70th Tank Battalion*. Binghamton, NY: Ty'ava Productions, 2008.

Ross, Francis, veteran of the 70th Tank Battalion, World War II. Conversations with author, 2009–15.

Service Company. Diary. 70th Tank Battalion. Roberts Armory Collection.

Taynton, Lewis, veteran of the 70th Tank Battalion, World War II. Conversations with author, 1995.

Tomasheski, Anthony I. Individual Deceased Personnel File.

Uttridge, Sarah. *Tanks and Armored Fighting Vehicles*. London: Amber Books, 2009.

Zaloga, Steven. *Armored Attack 1944*. Mechanicsburg, PA: Stackpole Books, 2011.

———. *The Sherman at War*. Hong Kong: Concord, 2000.

———. *U.S. Half-tracks of World War Two*. London: Lionel Leventhal, 1985.

———. *U.S. Tank Battles in France 1944–45*. Hong Kong: Concord, 2003.

Zaloga, Steven, and George Balin. *D-Day Tank Warfare*. Hong Kong: Concord, 1994.

Acknowledgments

I AM GRATEFUL to the following families and individuals who contributed photographs of the 70th Tank Battalion in World War II: Brodie, Ciaravella, Connors (Raimann), DeCarlo (Mundt), Dixon, Erickson (Poniatowski), Fritz, Gouget, Hallett, Isaacs, Kleinhuizen, Knoebel, Mary Lee Konty, McAtee, McKitrick (Larson), Malatesta, Ross, Stubbings, Taynton, Tomasheski, and Turner.

I am also grateful to the following individuals who were consulted and contributed to the writing of this work: Niels Henkemans (historian, specialist U.S. and German armor, Normandy, World War II), Sean Claxton (historian, Normandy, World War II), Richard Drew (Atlantic Wall historian, World War II), Robert Allen Dail Jr. (North Africa and Sicily historian, World War II), Jeff Wszolek (armor historian, World War II), and Mike Krizsanitz (historian, World War II).